BE IN THE TOP 1%

A REAL ESTATE AGENT'S GUIDE TO GETTING RICH IN THE INVESTMENT PROPERTY NICHE

BOB HELMS
"THE GODFATHER OF REAL ESTATE"

ISBN: 978-0-9983125-9-0

Printed in the United States of America.

DEDICATION

I am especially grateful that my parents, Budd and Grace Helms, provided such a loving family atmosphere for their children and gave my siblings and me the best opportunity they could provide for us to learn to cherish education and to accept the responsibility for our actions. My wife Dorothy and I were blessed to continue to live near and interact with my brother Bill, my sisters DeLoyce and JoAnne, and their entire families. It is an even greater blessing that all those aunts, uncles, and cousins are today good friends who treasure each other's company. I could hardly ask for more!

I am also very grateful for the opportunity to have worked closely with Robert Helms and Russell Gray, also known as The Real Estate Guys™, who for over 21 years have provided the best real estate investment education to their worldwide radio audience in over 190 countries. Perhaps I'm most proud that both Robert and Russ' family members call me "Papa."

Thank you to my many friends who have encouraged and inspired me to write this book. I am hopeful that it will garner the attention of and, more importantly, have an impact on the realtors and investors who can benefit from the ideas I have shared.

PRAISE FOR *BE IN THE TOP 1%*

"The very first commission I made selling real estate became the down payment on my first investment property, and my life was forever changed. That only happened through the teaching, encouragement and guidance of the man we affectionately call The Godfather of Real Estate. Full disclosure: he's my Dad, and I've been blessed to have him as my business partner, real estate mentor and investment advisor. Now his great wisdom can empower you as well. Read this book right away and change your financial life for the better!"

Robert Helms, Host, The Real Estate Guys™ Radio Show

"I have known Bob Helms for years, and when he has something to say, I listen. I listen because he has been practicing real estate for decades, and he has more experience than most people I know. If you want to speed up your wealth, you must learn from those more experienced. Bob Helms has both wisdom and experience that can only come from years of actually doing real estate deals. My suggestion is that you buy this book and read it often because it could be the difference between you being an average or top performer."

Ken McElroy, CEO, MC Companies, Rich Dad Advisor

"Bob Helms is the real deal. He has been masterfully living the lessons contained in this book for seven decades. If you want to become a top-selling agent, get this book and simply follow everything it says."

Monick Halm, Founder of Real Estate Investor Goddesses, MF Syndicator

"Bob Helms, The Godfather of Real Estate, gives the secret for those in real estate to create long-term wealth. This is something that is truly a gift to give to yourself and to those you know who want to go beyond selling real estate and actually own real estate, leveraging other people's time and money to create wealth. As my mentor Jim Rohn said, you can make a living or you can become wealthy, it all just gets down to the decisions you make and the philosophy you choose. Thanks Bob for sharing the roadmap."

Kyle Wilson, Founder of Jim Rohn International & KyleWilson.com

"A big challenge for me is finding an agent who truly understands property investment, and wants to take on 5+ seven-figure deals per year. This book is pure gold! I'm going to hand it out to every agent that wants to work with me."

Pete "The Deal Hunta" Halm, Syndicator, Investor

"Having seven decades of experience in real estate investing is rare, however, what makes Bob really special is his unselfish and limitless gift for sharing his wisdom with anyone who is astute enough to learn from his wealth of priceless lessons. I am fortunate to have had Bob in my life for many years, and I am very excited that his wonderful lessons and poignant humor are now being shared with you through this book!"

Tom Wilson, Radio Show Host, Long-Term Syndicator and Real Estate Investor

"Bob Helms has been a real estate investor longer than anyone I know. He not only has invested for his own portfolio but he also has served as an advisor, educator, and mentor to lots of up-and-coming investors. Bob personally looked over my shoulder and advised me on my first few multi-family apartment deals and helped me build a good foundation as an investor. This is a must read book for any real estate agent or broker who wants to secure their financial future by investing in cash flow real estate."

Dave Zook, The Real Asset Investor™, Syndicator, multi-class investor

"Hey real estate agents! You're leaving money on the table! Read this book and learn about a tremendous opportunity you are missing. You could take your income and business to the next level in the process. You are already in the game. This book will show you how to step your game up and lead you to opportunities most of your competitors don't even know exist!"

Dana Samuelson, Pres., American Gold Exchange

"If you're a real estate agent who wants more business, this book tells you how the investment property niche is substantially underserved today. Investor-clients transact more often and for higher purchase prices than homeowners. Bob Helms brilliantly reveals perhaps the biggest secret in all of real estate—the massive opportunity agents have to serve real estate investors."

Keith Weinhold, Founder and Owner GETRICHEDUCATION.COM, Host of One of America's Top Investing Shows

"As a high volume real estate investor, I totally sympathize with Bob's frustrations that the investor is the most underserved subset of real estate buyers. If you want average-Joe success, do what every Joe does (and pay for pay-per-click advertising) and market to average-Joe clients. If you want to get rich in the niche, read this book to go a mile-deep, inch-wide on your way to transform your business and financial outlook."

Lane Kawaoka, Real Estate Podcast host, Syndicator, Investor

"FINALLY! A Realtor that not only "gets it" but is willing to share "it" with others! As an investor, I know firsthand how hard it is to find a Realtor that is not only great at what they do but who also truly understands what I need from the inside out. The first question I ask a new Realtor or agent is, Do you invest in real estate for yourself? If they answer no then they can't truly understand what is important to me and how I think about things. Bob's book is a fountain of wisdom from years of experience and a must read for every agent or broker who wants to grow their career exponentially. Thank you, Bob, for sharing your wisdom!"

Gene Guarino, CFP, RALS, Founder, Residential Assisted Living Academy

"The most successful businesses solve real problems. In this enlightening book, Bob Helms, The Godfather of Real Estate, unlocks the secrets and his wealth of experience to help you solve the investor's problem of continually finding more income-producing properties. With Bob's help, it's easier than you think, especially when you realize you can become your own best client!"

Paula Brooks, Founder of FinancialFreedomFaster.com

"The key to becoming the top 1% is getting repeat business. Choose clients that bring repeat business every month instead of every decade. Bob's decades of first hand, practical experience provides a timeless guide on how to thrive in market up-cycles and down-cycles. Transforming from broker to trusted advisor forges client relationships for life. Let The Godfather be your guide."

Victor Menasce, Real Estate Investor, Developer, Syndicator, Author

FOREWORD

by Tom Hopkins

During my career in real estate, I learned way too many lessons the hard way. My only mode of transportation was a motorcycle. I was renting a studio apartment. I had no existing buyers and didn't know how to list property. And to top it off, I didn't know how to fill out any of the necessary paperwork to make an offer on a property. In fact, for my first sale, the buyer, who had purchased homes before, helped me fill out the paperwork.

There are plenty of quotes and sayings about experience being a great teacher, and I believe that to be true. However, experience is not the best teacher. Other people's experience is the best teacher—and the lessons are a lot less painful.

Early in my career, a fabulous speaker came to our real estate office and said something that not only stuck with me, but something I acted on. His words were, "You will make a great living on the commissions you'll earn selling real estate, but you'll create true wealth by investing in real estate." I took his words to heart and set a goal to start buying investment properties.

At first, I had little money to work with, but I found a few investors and offered to do all the leg work in exchange for an opportunity to share in the investment and then to manage the properties for them. (I could write a whole book myself on the lessons learned as a property manager. It's not for the faint of heart!) However, this experience gave me a way to leverage my career into something bigger. Because of my due diligence and working well with the numbers, my investors were pleased with their returns and were always ready to buy more.

I still did typical real estate transactions helping families find homes they would stay in for five to seven years, but that required working with a larger number of buyers. Simple math showed me that having a list of investors who trusted me and who were ready to buy properties almost as fast as I could find them would help me build personal wealth much faster. Eventually, I was in a position to invest wholly in properties on my own and did so extensively.

Bob Helms recognized the opportunities of working with investors early in his career as well. Bob, however, has taken real estate investing to a level I never dreamed of! I'm thrilled he's finally decided to share his incredible knowledge on this subject with today's real estate professionals.

I met Bob a few years back and liked him immediately. His laid-back manner, light heart, and smile make him pretty likeable. Behind that easy-going demeanor, though, is an analytical mind like no other when it comes to investing in real estate.

Working with investors is a niche within the real estate industry that is tremendously underserved. You will earn the equivalent of a master's degree in successful real estate investing—for yourself and others—within these pages. This book contains a wealth of other people's experiences for you to learn from...and gain tremendous benefit from. Treat it like the textbook it is. Understanding the formulas alone will put you ahead of 90% of other real estate agents when it comes to working with investors (or becoming one yourself).

Tom Hopkins, Bestselling Author, Acclaimed Trainer of Champion Real Estate Agents

TABLE OF CONTENTS

CHAPTER ONE

Getting Rich in the Investment Property Specialist Niche

It is absolutely amazing to me how many investors realize that this is an extraordinary time to begin or expand their real estate investment holdings, while most real estate agents are missing this golden opportunity. Very few real estate agents understand that they also have the opportunity to EXCEL as the investor's personal agent by handling all his investment property transactions—and that they can become wealthy by providing the services the investor desperately needs.

Does that mean that investors are much smarter than real estate agents? Hmm...not necessarily, but it definitely shows that while investors are focused on today's income property opportunities, real estate agents are not! Agents are rarely taught or encouraged to pursue a career specializing in serving investors who buy investment properties. Why do you think that is?

I believe it's because the agent's managers and owners before them rarely ever specialized in investment properties themselves. Even if those managers and owners are investors themselves, virtually none of them encourage their agents to select the investment property niche as a career choice, even on a part-time basis. The result is that agents do not become investment property specialists, which means that they do not participate in one of the BEST opportunities available to them as service providers to the thousands of investors who desperately need their help!

I also believe this oversight commonly results in what I would call a career tragedy for real estate agents, for two reasons:

1. Real estate agents are not participating in this very lucrative segment of the market where they have essentially no competition

from other agents! The investment property segment is so poorly served that investors are desperate to find and work with knowledgeable agents. There are just so few of them around! There is a great demand for investment property specialists, and everything you need to know to succeed in this arena is easily within reach.

2. Not learning to become an investment property specialist will cause real estate agents to miss the opportunity to become an investor themselves, thereby missing the opportunity to provide an extraordinary lifestyle for themselves, and ultimately providing very handsomely for their retirement.

How Can YOU Become an Investment Property Specialist (IPS)?

First, let us acknowledge that there is no official designation by the National Association of Realtors (or anyone else) of an investment property specialist, or IPS. So whether you choose to think that an IPS is an INVESTMENT property specialist, or you think an IPS is an INCOME property specialist doesn't matter...You are right! You can call yourself whatever you like when you decide to specialize in helping investors become more successful and let their successes become your successes in the process. I have personally been calling myself an investment property specialist for the 38+ years I've been a practicing real estate broker.

No matter what you call yourself, it is absolutely possible for YOU to become the valuable agent that investors want to assist them—again and again—while they build their portfolio of investment properties. **Don't miss this key point:** If you decide to serve the investor community, you will indeed become a far busier agent because investors buy, sell, and own many more properties than residential clients!

The top one percent of real estate agents in America are regularly earning six-figure incomes. You can do the same if you learn how to become an investment property specialist who knows how to assist your investor clients in achieving their investment goals. Unlike those other top-earning real estate agents, you will also be building an investment property portfolio that can provide equal or much greater earnings when you're ready to retire from your sales career and let your properties work for you!

If you've ever considered becoming an investor or assisting the many investors who see the opportunities and are buying these properties, you will likely never have a better time to start than right now!

You can learn to participate in investment property transactions that will give you the experience you need to become an investor yourself, which in turn, will help you build a portfolio of properties for your own retirement. When you own real estate yourself, your credibility as an investment property specialist will increase quickly, and you can become the "go to" agent in your office...or town!

And, it's easier than you think! This is an opportunity for you to step up and learn to get rich in a niche! Here's why this opportunity exists and why NOW is the right time to take advantage of it:

If you're like most real estate agents in America, you know very little about investing in real estate. You probably do not own investment properties, and you don't understand exactly how those properties are valued. In your real estate career thus far, you have had very few role models to emulate in learning how to get rich in the investment property real estate niche.

Why do you suppose MOST real estate agents don't pursue this niche?

Do you think that's because it's a crowded, competitive marketplace?

IT'S NOT!

Is it because it's a very difficult, hard-to-learn, segment of the business?

IT'S NOT!

Is it because there's less opportunity to participate in these transactions?

NO, THERE IS MORE!

Let me illustrate. According to the California Association of Realtors (with approximately 500,000 agent members), only five percent of real estate agents (that's 1 out of every 20) will be involved in more than one investment property transaction in their ENTIRE CAREER! Does that sound like stiff competition? No, of course not...and it does not require a CCIM[1] to understand the transaction model, either.

[1] A CCIM (Certified Commercial Investment Member) is a recognized expert in the commercial and investment real estate industry.

So, do you believe that California is the ONLY place where real estate agents don't participate in the investment property market? Is it the only state where agents don't understand the benefits of focusing on serving the investors who want and need their help? No, of course not!

The investor community is underserved throughout the United States, as it is throughout most of the world! Does it sound like there just may be a tremendous opportunity for you to participate in this business?

If you're an active agent, chances are good that you've already worked with investors who are buying single-family homes as investments, and they'll buy more if they have the capacity to do so. And, YOU can be bringing them the deals, but only if you learn how to be a valued team member to these clients. If you become an agent who knows how to find, analyze, and present the opportunities to these clients they'll want YOU to be their investment property agent because of these deals and your skills.

Now, here's the really good news. Unlike the non-investor clients who already know you, like you, and trust you, but only use your services when they move every five to seven years, investor clients can do transactions whenever you find a property that meets their needs and desires. No waiting! YOU determine the timing and the amount of business you do in this arena because you can CREATE transactions that wouldn't take place without you!

As you build up a clientele of investors, you can easily create transactions between those clients. By understanding their individual goals and their property acquisition plans and strategies, you are able to provide exceptional service by helping them achieve the results they desire. It's NOT hard.

And, you have very little competition from other agents for this business because 19 out of 20 of them don't know how to provide the services these investors need!

▶ NOTE

Although there are no definite limitations on the size and value of the properties you handle for your investor clients, the "sweet spot" for properties that are below a commercial agent's radar is probably less than $10,000,000. That means these properties are generally too small for the commercial broker and his clients, but just right for mom and pop, newer investors, and those who are serious about increasing their net worth.

Here's Great Advice For Real Estate Agents: "Become Your Own Best Client!"

America's legendary real estate agent and sales trainer, Mr. Tom Hopkins, suggests that you become your own best customer. Tom says, "You can make a good living selling real estate to others, but you can make a fortune if you buy some for yourself!"

Tom gave that same advice to my son Robert Helms in 1987 when Robert was a green real estate agent just entering the business, and Robert readily embraced Tom's ideas. Today, Robert is a successful real estate developer building multimillion dollar projects. He also hosts the acclaimed *The Real Estate Guys™* radio program for investors, a show that reaches 190+ countries and educates thousands of listeners about the many ways to succeed in real estate investing.

▶ NOTE

Here's a hint: The show is a great resource for investors and agents, so go to the website at www.RealEstateGuysRadio.com and start listening!

It's A Secret

This investment property real estate niche is completely underpopulated by real estate agents—just as it has been for the 38 years I've been an investment property specialist—and its existence is still a viable, well-kept secret from most agents today! So, if you find this idea intriguing, how do you learn the skills necessary to succeed in this niche? Happily, almost everything you need to know is presented in this book!

If you're a real estate beginner, you'll need to learn the basics of real estate sales while you also learn about investment properties. If you're a seasoned real estate professional, it'll be simpler for you because you already understand the rudiments of the real estate sales business. You know how to work with buyers and sellers, so you can focus on learning to deal with investment properties.

Imagine...

Just imagine what it's like to be a new real estate investor today. She's learning how the business is done. She's very excited and she starts looking for a good agent to be a key member of her team...but 19 out of 20 candidates cannot help her! What must she do? Well, I'm afraid she will have to kiss a LOT of frogs before she finds the right agent, because agents who can help her are very few-and-far-between. Investors absolutely need the services of a qualified agent, and there are virtually NO LIMITS on how much business that agent can do as they improve their skills and understanding of this marketplace.

And...do you suppose there just might be a huge opportunity for you to solicit investment property client referrals from successful agents specializing in home sales? Remember, they don't understand investment properties, but they DO understand referral fees...especially on transactions they cannot do by themselves. Your job is to make sure they know you are an available, competent professional, you will treat their referral clients very well, and you will endorse them for referring business to you. It becomes a win-win for everyone, while helping you build your reputation and your own real estate portfolio!

Of course, it's quite possible for you to gain those referrals by helping other agents become interested in investing, too. They can assist you with the client referrals they provide, or refer themselves to you as clients who want to learn how to become investors.

Let's Summarize Why This May Be the Best Opportunity You've Ever Seen

A virtually unknown opportunity exists today for real estate agents to become immensely successful by focusing on serving clients who are real estate investors. This opportunity is open to both beginners and seasoned agents, and does not require that you abandon your current practice working with homebuyers and homesellers. This new segment of your business can be in addition to your owner-occupied client transactions, and can quickly propel you to becoming an expert, sought-after investment property specialist! Even more importantly, you will also learn how to become your own best client and to build your own investment property portfolio!

What Does It Take for YOU to Become an Investment Property Specialist?

That depends upon how much, if any, exposure you've had to working with investors and investment properties to date. The most important factor will be your motivation and your commitment to investing the time and effort required to learn how it's done. Don't worry about what you don't know, because every skill you'll need can indeed be learned, and no one was born with the necessary skill sets of an investment property specialist!

So just what ARE the skills you must master to become a successful investment property specialist? What do you have to learn to distinguish yourself from all those other real estate agents who are helping homebuyers and home sellers complete their transactions? In order to serve investors effectively, you must learn to think like an investor and to view investment properties the same way an investor does. To do this, you will have to learn to "speak income!" Every business is unique, with unique terminology and vocabulary used in day-to-day discussions and transactions, and you need to become familiar with the language of investing.

To speak income fluently, you'll want to know exactly how to do what successful real estate investors do:

1. Understand the many investing options available to real estate investors and put together a PLAN that allows you to determine exactly what you want your investments to do for you. Once you do this, you will often be able to assist your investors in the same preparation, because many investors have not done such an analysis. By helping them, you'll be able to add value to their preparation and improve their results. (See Chapter Three: Understanding Investment Properties)

2. Analyze a rental property's performance to determine whether it fits the criteria in your plan. If not, you may want to consider improving the property so that it will perform well enough for you or your client. (See Chapter Four: Valuing Investment Properties)

3. Build and manage your growing portfolio of properties to ensure that you can accomplish your retirement goals. This includes selecting the right vehicles to provide the results you want from the investment properties you choose to own and operate. (See Chapter Six: How Do You Build And Manage a Real Estate Portfolio Successfully?)

4. Develop an understanding of the tax benefits of owning investment properties. You don't need to be a CPA, but you'll need to learn what benefits are available for investors and how to employ them. Your government created a tax code which strongly incentivizes investment, and you need to know how investors can benefit by taking advantage of those incentives. (See Chapter Five: Tax Benefits of Owning Real Estate)

By learning these and a few other essential skills, you will soon find yourself "speaking income" more and more fluently and realizing it's not that difficult! We will also address a critical set of skills that will help you become a successful real estate agent! (See Chapter Nine: Preparing to Become a Uniquely Successful Real Estate Agent)

One shortcut to learning new skills is to study how successful practitioners perform; let's take a look at the business model used by me and my son, investment property specialists Bob and Robert Helms.

Bob and Robert were an active father-and-son real estate team for 18 years. Most of those years were spent working in a large, California residential real estate company, where Bob helped manage one of their larger offices for many years. Because they were also long-term investors, they specialized in working the investment property real estate niche, and 35-40% of their total business regularly came from investor transactions. They also enjoyed and pursued referrals from agents in their office and other offices, because they established a successful track record servicing and completing transactions with those referral clients...resulting in referral fees for the agents, and new clients for Bob and Robert. They were also able to help several agents start their own investment careers and begin building retirement portfolios for themselves.

Don't miss this key point: Bob and Robert were long-term real estate investors themselves, which gave them both a greater understanding of the marketplace and immediate credibility as local income property experts. Their personal real estate holdings included condominiums, single-family homes, duplexes, several apartment buildings, a medical-dental building and a commercial warehouse, so they had considerable experience owning and operating different types of income-producing properties. Bob and Robert understood what their clients needed and how to serve them.

The major reason for you to become your client's investment property expert is because you will then understand how and why investment properties provide unparalleled opportunities for those investors to become wealthy and why you will want to join them as an investor yourself—as soon are you are able to participate. As soon as you become your own best client, and start buying properties for your own portfolio, your credibility as an investment property specialist increases dramatically, as does your value to your clients. There is essentially no limit to the amount of business you can generate in this virtually competition-free environment.

Some Advantages of Becoming an Investment Property Specialist

1. As you begin to build your own property portfolio, several benefits will accrue. Your credibility as an investment property specialist will continue to increase as you are able to understand more about the niche and communicate more effectively with your clients. You bring more value to the relationship.

2. Your earnings from your rental properties will continue to increase, and will ultimately provide significant cash flow to supplement your commissioned income.

3. Your real estate investment business will also provide significant tax benefits of ownership that allow you to keep considerably more of what you've earned. One of the most compelling reasons to invest in real estate in America (and most other countries) is

that your government recognizes that offering tax incentives for you to help provide housing or office space for others is the surest way to get you to participate.

▶ **NOTE**

We will examine the tax benefits of owning investment properties in greater detail in Chapter Five: Tax Benefits of Owning Real Estate.

Don't Keep It a Secret

A key element of achieving success in your career as a real estate agent is that you don't keep what you do a secret! Get in the habit of making sure your friends, associates, and prospects ALL know that you're an agent, and that you SPECIALIZE in helping investors buy and sell investment properties. Your goal is NOT to be average and ordinary; it is to stand out as one who delivers superb service, which you cannot do anonymously. You need to consciously build your brand while you build your skills, and continually search for ways to bring value to your clients.

Elevator Speech

How do you get the attention of others to tell them what you do? One of the simplest and most effective ways is to perfect and use your "elevator speech" to quickly tell people WHO you are, WHAT you do, WHAT you are interested in doing, and HOW you can be a resource to them!

This is hard to do on the spot unless you have carefully prepared and condensed a description of you and your business in advance. Rehearse your elevator speech until you can do it easily without a warmup! Don't waste the opportunity to connect with others by not being prepared. You can sound confident, focused, and knowledgeable…or muddled and confused. Remember, you only get ONE chance to make a positive first impression.

You must be able to communicate who you are and what you offer your clients. Potential investor clients will appreciate learning quickly whether you and they have sufficient common interests to initiate a dialogue.

Make sure that your 30-60 second elevator speech includes the key things you do, e.g., "I specialize in helping real estate investors make good decisions when buying, selling, and managing their properties."

Of course, a prepared agent and investor will ALWAYS have business cards available to facilitate follow up with new prospects!

Write a Newspaper Column or a Blog

While Bob and Robert were active real estate investment specialists, they wrote a column entitled "Ask The Realtors" for a local newspaper which served them very well because they received quality leads from their readers and notoriety from the exposure in their marketplace. They selected topics of general interest to homebuyers, home sellers, and investors that would answer some questions, while provoking further questions, and invited these readers to call or email them with those questions. They also referred the readers to Robert's radio show, The Real Estate Guys™, for timely discussions of interesting real estate topics.

Today, the radio show is heard worldwide, and Robert continues to repeat his "Ask The Guys" segment to answer his listener's best investment questions.

Here are some of the titles they featured in the newspaper column:

- "You Have Income Property to Sell...What Are Your Options?"
- "It's a Great Time to Invest in Real Estate."
- "How Can You Get the Best Price Selling Your Home?"
- "Will Rising Interest Rates Cool Off this Hot Marketplace?"
- "Why Do Over 20% of all 1031 Tax-Deferred Exchanges Fail?"
- "Megan's Law – Another Very Important Disclosure Between Buyers and Sellers"

The articles ended with a short descriptive paragraph about the authors:

> *Bob and Robert Helms are Realtors associated with Century 21 Seville Contempo Realty. Their experience encompasses first-time buyers, new and resale homes, tax-deferred exchanges of income properties, and property management. Written questions can be mailed to: Bob and Robert Helms (c/o Ask The Realtors), 1096 Blossom Hill Road #200, San Jose, CA 95123. Telephone is: (408) 690-5512*
>
> *Email is: bhelms@finehomesandestates.com*

So, while this may not be the most remarkable marketing campaign you've ever seen, let's examine what it DID accomplish and why it was effective for Bob and Robert:

1. First and foremost, they specialized in and actively solicited business and relationships with investors, while continuing to do 60 to 65% of their total business with homebuyers and homesellers. Yes, they were active in both arenas, but always made it clear that they were a team that could ably assist both groups.

2. Writing the column definitely enhanced their professional image and provided credibility with their real estate peers and with their company's management. Very few other agents took advantage of the opportunity this afforded, and it therefore positioned them differently from the average agent.

   The company Bob and Robert worked for was ranked as the 25th largest residential real estate company IN AMERICA at that time. They operated 17 offices and effectively dominated their marketplace, yet only five or six of those offices had agents who were investment property specialists. (Translation: Less than one third of the offices and only a handful of agents company-wide were able to "speak income" fluently).

3. **Note the topic of the first question posed above:**

   "You have income property to sell...what are your options?"

   Who is going to READ this article?

   Primarily people with income property to sell....

   That's good, because those are exactly the people they were trying to reach with that question!

Bob and Robert also engaged the services of a mortgage lender and a local CPA to help them conduct small seminars in the evenings and on weekends at their company's offices entitled "Build Your Real Estate Empire." These didn't exactly rival a Tom Hopkins event (with an average of only 5 to 20 attendees), but they continued to build their brand and their reputation, as they found new investor clients, one by one. Robert went on to become an outstanding seminar presenter, attracting hundreds of investors to his presentations, and he continues doing so today.

Robert came up with another interesting way to prospect for clients that utilized some of his personal skills and professional talents outside of his real estate business. Robert's musical skills took two avenues; he played guitar in a rock group, and he also had experience as a live, on-air radio host, and as a portable DJ providing music for hundreds of weddings and private parties. Those DJ experiences introduced him to wedding fairs which featured all the services and service providers a new bride and groom would need for their wedding ceremony and related events.

Because Robert had appeared at several wedding fairs as a DJ, he proposed that Bob & Robert Helms, Realtors®, should host a booth at an upcoming wedding fair, offering a drawing to win a free DJ for their wedding or party. This gave them the opportunity to get acquainted with these prospective new clients while they filled out their contest entry forms, and to offer them a free audio tape which Robert and Bob had recorded called "Buying Your First Home."

This campaign wasn't designed to produce any investors, of course, but they did connect with several prospective homebuyers, and the cost of participating in the wedding fair was regained many times over. They continued to use the audio tape to educate first-time buyers for many more years. It was unique, and it produced results!

We've included this example of Robert's creative marketing approach to finding additional new clients to illustrate that YOU, too, can succeed by thinking about what unique tool or talent you can employ to create new business prospects. Don't be afraid to experiment; people are attracted to ideas that are unique and not commonplace. Having collateral materials that YOU have produced lends credibility and professionalism to your presentations.

Of course, there are any number of ways to grow yourself into an investment property specialist. What's important for you to understand here, is that it's relatively easy to do, and the lack of qualified agents serving this marketplace virtually guarantees your opportunity to succeed.

Are You Afraid You Might Be TOO YOUNG to Be a Believable IPS?

People should not judge you by how you look...but they do, so it's important that you always dress appropriately. But that certainly does NOT mean that you have to don a wig to look old enough to be "believable" as an IPS. What you DO need to do is learn your trade and be able to speak intelligently about the issues and facts that interest the investors you work with.

Investors, like everybody else, may defer to the gray-haired oldster whom they presume has been an IPS forever until they open their mouth and reveal whether they "speak income" fluently or not! Adequate maturity in understanding investment properties is not about age, but about education, and I've never met an investor who would trade expertise for a lack thereof when selecting an IPS to work with.

Let me illustrate the importance of an IPS' education by telling you about a couple of investor friends of mine, Tracey and Justin, who have been expanding their investment portfolio for many years, but like most other investors, have had great difficulty finding IPSs who speak income over the years. Tracey and Justin finally resorted to printing a business card just for agents, which lists the formulas needed to calculate the major parameters they will require to evaluate an income property...*because most agents don't know those formulas or even know why they are important!* Believe me, Tracey and Justin don't care about the IPS' age... only his or her ability! If you have a real estate license, you are old enough to become an IPS!

And of course, if you ARE a more mature individual, who might be beginning his or her second career (I became a real estate agent at age 45) and you are new to real estate sales, you probably WILL get the benefit of the doubt when you meet new clients.... They WILL assume you've been at this business for a while, so it's not necessary for you to immediately proclaim your rookie status! Of course, you never lie to people about your experience—or anything else—because you are seeking to build a relationship of trust with them, but your "seniority" is valid and your life experiences have prepared you to focus on what clients need. You ARE more mature, so it's fair that you enjoy the benefits of your maturity.

In Chapter Two: Lessons Learned From My First Investment Property Transaction as a Real Estate Agent, I'll share with you the advantages I had as a 45-year-old beginner—because I was both older, and I was already an experienced real estate investor. I'll also share why that transaction proved to be a much bigger lesson than I anticipated, because I made a serious rookie mistake that could have cost me my new real estate license!

Becoming an IPS will take hard work for anyone new to the business, but any worthwhile endeavor will require your dedication, your energy and a commitment to stick with the program until you reach your goal of becoming a significant force as an investment property specialist. When you accomplish that, you will have no limitations on your ability to succeed, other than those you place on yourself.

You will likely never have a better time to start than RIGHT NOW!

Recommended Reading List

1. *Equity Happens* by Robert Helms & Russell Gray
2. *How to Master the Art of Selling* by Tom Hopkins
3. *Rich Dad, Poor Dad* by Robert Kiyosaki
4. *The ABC's of Real Estate Investing* by Ken McElroy
5. *Second Chance* by Robert Kiyosaki
6. *Escape The Madness* by Gena Lofton
7. *Park Place: How to Cash In on the Mobile Home Park Niche* by Tony Ferris
8. *Investing in Real Estate* by Dr. Gary Eldred

Other Resources for Real Estate Investors

The Real Estate Guys™ weekly radio show for investors—download the podcasts from their website at www.RealEstateGuysRadio.com or subscribe to the show on iTunes.

CHAPTER TWO

Lessons Learned From My First Investment Property Transaction as a Real Estate Agent

Why would the story of my first investment property transaction as a real estate agent be sufficiently noteworthy to include in a book aimed at coaching aspiring investment property specialists and investors? Because while there certainly are some practical lessons to be gained by "looking over an agent's shoulder" for a transaction, there is a much bigger lesson in understanding the details of an important mistake I made as a rookie agent in that first transaction. The nature of any business is that we will make mistakes, and we will often pay a high price for those lessons. When we do, we definitely want to get the lesson. To err is human. When we get the lesson, we can recover and move on.

I learned many lessons from my first transaction as a real estate agent, and those lessons were not just about the property. Let me review how and why I became an agent whose first deal was representing the buyers of a six-unit apartment building, and why I was lucky to survive this transaction and retain my broker's license!

Real estate sales is my second career, which I began at age 45, following a 20-year journey as a high-tech sales and marketing manager for several Silicon Valley companies in the San Francisco Bay area. I was, by this time, an experienced investor, and I owned a number of rental properties. My brother was a civil engineer, working as the engineering manager for a local city, and we invested in several properties together. We owned single-family homes, duplexes, fourplexes, several small apartment buildings, a medical-dental building and a 50-unit apartment building near San Jose State University. My wife, Dorothy, managed the properties, and without any real guidance or mentoring, we were lucky enough to establish a nice portfolio of local properties which provided sufficient cash flow to allow us to continue to invest.

We actually bought our first property while I was still an engineering student at San Jose State University, so the job of property manager defaulted to Dorothy, who fortunately had the necessary skills and aptitude to become an excellent PM, a job which she handled very well for many years.

Becoming a Realtor®

At no time while building an investment property portfolio, did I ever consider becoming a realtor®, until a neighbor of mine opened a new real estate office and approached me to help her handle investment properties. As an agent who owned investment properties herself, Doris was successful enough, and ambitious enough, to open a new office. She knew I was also an investor and was certain I understood enough about investing to help her generate a business segment specifically for investors.

While it would be nice to profess that I was intrigued by Doris' unique idea of creating a company that specialized in serving investors, I was actually pretty clueless about the dearth of agents working in this arena. I wasn't sufficiently educated to even understand just how unique her idea was, and at that point, I didn't understand that most investors were desperate to find a good investment property specialist.

In truth, I was flattered that she approached me, but I wasn't very interested at first. I was certainly not willing to give up my job as a well-paid regional sales representative for a Los Angeles electronics company, but in reality, the sales job didn't really require my full-time attention. Because my employer was manufacturing custom parts for a limited number of applications, and wasn't interested in expanding, I eventually decided that I could work at real estate part-time. So I got my broker's license and started to learn how to play the investment property real estate game from Doris, her new broker, John, and a couple of other "old salts" who joined the team.

Doris' broker, John, was also an investor, and he and his wife Barbara worked with many investors, so I was sure he'd teach me the things I needed to know about real estate in general, and income properties in particular. Of course, I learned some lessons I hadn't anticipated!

John had just listed a six-unit apartment building, which had a vacant unit, so we were able to see it on the office tour. For those of you who aren't yet agents, most real estate offices have weekly tours to enable their agents to see the newly listed properties. This helps prepare them to intelligently discuss the properties with prospective buyers who call responding to the ads the brokerage runs specifically to attract such calls. The "floor agent" (the agent answering the incoming call, usually on a rotational basis) is trained to get an appointment with the caller to show them the property, with the hope of being able to write an offer if the caller is sufficiently interested. (Many residential real estate offices don't include rental properties on their office tours, but this company was established to service investors, and therefore listed and promoted both homes and investment properties).

Normally, rental properties are occupied by tenants, so agents aren't able to preview them, and offers are therefore written subject to inspection, meaning the offer is subject to the buyer's physical walk-through inspection shortly after an offer to purchase is accepted by the seller. This walkthrough is considered a Go - No Go inspection, and the buyer must agree that the property is satisfactory (essentially, what he expected based upon his view from outside the property), and remove the initial inspection contingency, if he wants to proceed with the transaction. If he does not approve, the contract is either withdrawn/cancelled, or the buyer can choose to modify the offer, based on his walk-through inspection. If buyer and seller agree to proceed with the transaction, the buyer will then order and pay for additional inspections by local service companies, who will perform property inspections, termite inspections, and perhaps structural, roof, foundation or other inspections, as are appropriate. Each inspector furnishes a written report so that buyer and seller have the same information to work with when determining whether they will complete the transaction as written, agree to any work to be done (and at whose expense), and modify the contract, if necessary, before completion of the transaction. These inspections are part of what is called the buyer's due diligence requirement. Such Inspections can be waived, but unless you're planning to tear down the building(s), why wouldn't you learn as much as you can from professional craftsmen who understand the details that inspections reveal?

My First Floor Call

Back to the six-unit apartment. I was able to preview it (wearing my experienced investor's hat), and I surmised that it was in reasonable condition and was also very reasonably priced at $113,500. So, I was well prepared when I received my first "floor call" from a prospective buyer. I made an appointment to show him the property, subject to the availability of the vacant unit, and met with the buyer and his three partners at my new office. The four buyers were all Silicon Valley engineers, who had formed a new enterprise, Big Four Associates, specifically to invest in Bay Area apartment buildings. They were in the process of structuring a management entity to operate their rentals and were excited to get started. An important part of our meeting was taking time to understand who they were, what their objectives were, and making sure they understood that I had been personally investing in this same area for over 20 years, so I knew the marketplace well and I was able to provide the kind of expertise they needed to get started.

We met the listing agent, my broker, John, at the property, and he showed us the vacant unit, which was unfurnished, but clean, and included a gas stove with an oven, a refrigerator, wall-to-wall carpeting and a tiled tub-shower. The building also featured a laundry room and six carports, with a communal yard and BBQ area for the tenant's use. John was also acting as the property manager for the owner, and divulged that he had received a prospective tenant's application to rent the vacant unit. The buyer's were generally pleased with what they saw, with the exception of the building's outside painting, which they thought should be redone.

Before we left the property, I asked the buyer's to tell me their impression of the property and whether they thought it was a candidate for their first apartment building purchase.

They said it was definitely of interest, but they wanted to talk it over. We agreed to meet the following day to review the property's pro forma data and talk about how we could structure an offer, if they wanted to pursue it.

▶ NOTE

An experienced agent might not have left them to review their findings alone at this stage, but my instincts were to give them plenty of space. We were just establishing a relationship, and I made it clear that even though the property was listed for sale by my company—which owed an allegiance to the seller because he hired us to sell the property—my interest was to serve them, be it on this property or another property. My goal was to form a long-term relationship with investors who needed and would appreciate my insight and abilities. I wasn't looking for a single sale; I wanted to be their investment property specialist. I definitely recognized that this group had the ability and a plan to repeat this process many times!

I met with Big Four Associates the next day to review the pro forma data which John had prepared for us. The listing broker typically furnishes this pro forma for the buyer's team to review with disclaimers about its accuracy. (NOTE: It's important for the reader to understand that pro forma data is created with certain assumptions, and those assumptions DO NOT necessarily reflect the current performance of the property; pro forma data may assume different rents, new loans in place, etc., so, it is definitely not audited or certified information).

No physical inspections had been performed by the seller; If any inspection reports existed for the property, the seller should have furnished them to the buyer for review, although not necessarily before the parties entered into a contract for the building. If the buyers elected to purchase the units, any and all inspections desired would become their responsibility and would be performed at the buyer's expense.

They Like It and Want to Make an Offer!

The buyers decided to submit an offer for the units, so we spent a couple of hours reviewing the details and questions they had about the property and the process before writing their offer. We called a lender that John recommended who specialized in smaller apartment loans. The lender assured them that he could get them approved for a loan at competitive rates. I reviewed the terms of the proposed loan, and calculated the property's performance. The performance parameters would provide a net positive cash flow if purchased at the asking price.

▶ NOTE

Understanding how to perform a cash flow analysis on any income property is one of the skills that is critical for you to master and is covered in detail in Chapter Four: Valuing Investment Properties. You must get good at analyzing a property's performance to be able to provide key information for your investor clients and for yourself. The primary complaint we hear from investors is that the agents they have sought help from did not know how to make these calculations nor did they understand why the calculations were so important to the investor in his purchasing decision.

As is customary for properties with five units or more, the lender required a 30% down payment and agreed to lend them 70% of the purchase price, or the appraised value, whichever was less (a 70% loan-to-value, or LTV loan). Moreover, the property was required to produce a net operating income after paying all operating expenses of at least 1.2 times the new mortgage payment. This is called the debt coverage ratio, or DCR, and is very common for these type of loans. The buyer's personal credit is of paramount importance when obtaining conventional loans on properties of four units or less, but the property's performance is considered more important for five units or more.

Although the property performed well at the seller's asking price, the buyers wanted to offer less. We wrote the offer at approximately 10% below the asking price, offering $103,500. The buyers made an appointment to meet with the lender to complete a written loan application. This step allowed them to obtain a confirmation of the proffered loan terms, which meant that they could confidently remove their loan approval contingency when the lender received a satisfactory property appraisal.

▶ NOTE

Although I was pretty familiar with the offer to purchase (deposit receipt), my experiences using it were as a buyer or seller, not as an agent, so I prepared myself by reviewing other office transaction files to help me be ready to understand and answer the buyer's questions.

Presenting the Offer

I advised John that I had an offer to present. He set up an appointment with the seller, and although I didn't know it yet, I was in for a very pleasant surprise! At least I thought it was pleasant. When John introduced me to his seller, he turned out to be a man I already knew! He was a purchasing agent for one of the electronic companies I called on in my other job as a regional sales representative for a Los Angeles manufacturing company. What a small world!

I was allowed the opportunity to present the offer verbally, to John and the seller, which I think helped the seller appreciate that the buyers were credible, and that I was a seasoned investor, myself, so I'd be able to coach them through the transaction details. The seller wasn't thrilled with the price they offered, but I assured him these were ready, willing and able buyers whom he could count on to close the transaction. He then revealed that his purpose for selling the six units was to buy a bigger apartment building, and he was planning to do an IRS 1031 tax-deferred exchange. However, the offer we presented to him wouldn't allow him to complete that exchange, unless the price was adjusted to approximately 95% of the asking price. So John wrote a counter offer at $108,000, which also required the buyers to cooperate in affecting the seller's 1031 exchange. In this case, "cooperation" merely means that the buyers would help facilitate the title transfer of the exchange property during the transaction's closing.

I again met with Big Four Associates to discuss the terms of the counter-offer, and to recalculate the impact of the price change on the building's performance. We concluded that, at the new price of $108,000, the before tax cash flow (BTCF) would be approximately $247 per month, which definitely worked for the buyers.

▶ NOTE

Calculation of the property's cash flow analysis is detailed in Figure 1 A & B. This shows how we determine the buyer's before tax cash flow (BTCF) as well as several other performance indicators. In Chapter Four: Valuing Investment Properties, we will extend these calculations to include the buyer's estimated after tax cash flow (ATCF).

FIGURE 1 A & B

Analysis of Purchase and Operating Costs & Cash Flow Projections

Six-Unit Apartment Building for Big Four Associates

Purchase Price:	$108,000	Terms: 25 year, fixed rate, fully amortized.
Down Payment (30%):	$32,400	At 8.95% per annum = $632 per month,
New First Loan (70%):	$75,600	P&I Loan Cost is 2 Points = $1,512

Operating Expenses:

Property taxes:	$1,080 per year = $90 per month	(estimated at 1% of purchase price per year)
Insurance:	$898 per year = $74 per month	(estimate by local insurance agency)
Utilities:	$500 per year = $42 per month	(house only; tenants separately metered)
Accounting/Legal:	$400 per year = $34 per month	
Repair Allowance:	$1,440 per year = $120 per month	(estimated at $20 per unit per month)
Property Management:	$0 per year = $0 per month	(owners will self-manage the property rentals)

Total Operating Expenses: $4,318 per year = $360 per month

Projected Cash Flow

Projected Cash Flow is calculated using the **BASIC INCOME FORMULA:**

Calculate Gross Scheduled Income (GSI):

Income from Rental Units:

$14,400 per year = $1,200 per month (based on $200 per month per unit)

+ Income from Laundry Room:

$1,248 per year = $104 per month (based on $4 per week per unit)

Total GSI:	$15,648 per year	=	$1,304 per month
Vacancy & Bad Debt (5%):	– $782 per year	=	– $65 per month
Effective Gross Income (95%):	$14,866 per year	=	$1,239 per month
Less Operating Expenses:	– $4,318 per year	=	– $360 per month
Net Operating Income:	$10,548 per year	=	$879 per month
Less Debt Service:	– $7,582 per year	=	– $632 per month
Before Tax Cash Flow (BTCF):	$ 2,966 per year	=	$247 per month

This analysis has been performed by using the listing broker's estimates of the property's rental and laundry income plus some estimated expenses and the lender's estimates of the purchase loan parameters and costs. These allow us to anticipate the total amount of cash required to complete the purchase initially and to project the ongoing cash flow during operation of the property.

Initial Purchase expense is:	$32,400	Down Payment
	+ $1,512	Loan Points
	+ $1,700	Escrow/Title
Cash required to complete purchase:	$35,612	

One requirement of the purchase money loan is that the property produce adequate cash flow to meet the debt coverage ratio (DCR) which, in this case, is 1.2. This means that the net operating income must be at least 1.2 times the monthly principal and interest payment of the loan, or, 1.2 x $632 per month = $ 758.40 per month

With a net operating income (NOI) of $879 per month, the actual DCR is higher than the minimum required and, in fact, is: $879 ÷ $632 = 1.39, which exceeds the lender's required income to debt margin.

Before Tax Cash Flow = $247 per month x 12 months = $2,964 per year

Cash on Cash Return = $2964 ÷ $35,612 = 8.32% (cash return on initial cash invested)

GRM = $108,000 ÷ $15,648 = 6.9 (Gross Rent Multiplier (GRM) reveals price paid for property as a function of its annual income)

Cap Rate = NOI ÷ Purchase Price = $10,548 ÷ $108,000 = 9.7%

Cap rate is a percentage reflecting net return after expenses as a function of purchase price or FMV.

SUMMARY: The GRM and Cap rate are both strong, positive performance indicators in this case, and the pre-tax cash-on-cash return of 8.32% is also an acceptable return on investment for this group of investors.

Buyers Accept Sellers Counter-Offer – We Have A Deal!

The buyers decided to move ahead with the transaction, so they signed the counter-offer, removed their "walk-through" inspection contingency, and asked the seller to paint the outside of the building.

I called broker John to tell him, "We have a deal!" Wow! This was exciting!

So, we were ready to proceed with the purchase, and things were looking good so far! John the broker installed a key safe on the vacant unit to facilitate scheduling inspections, and I arranged for one or more of the buyers to attend the inspections, so they'd have the opportunity to get any questions answered while the inspectors were still on the premises.

By this time, I had become acquainted with some of Doris' other new agents (all "old salts" with a lot of experience dealing with investors and investment properties, and all definitely investment property specialists). So I was able to solicit and use their referrals to select and hire the local inspectors. It has been my habit of many years to personally attend all inspections, which allows me to ask questions of the inspectors, too. I highly recommend that, as an investment property specialist, you incorporate this step into your procedures, which will ensure that you are also knowledgeable about the property's condition.

The inspections were scheduled and completed, and happily, the buyers found nothing to be particularly concerned about. The building's plumbing and electrical systems were functional, the roof was estimated to have approximately 10-15 years remaining life, and the buyers were ready to move ahead, subject to getting their purchase loan approval.

Buyers Ready to Close, But Seller Drags His Feet

Because the buyers were very strong financially, their loan was routinely approved. We were now ready to go, but for some unknown reason, the seller began to drag his feet a little and didn't order the building to be painted as agreed. I tried to get John to pressure the seller to complete the painting so we could close the transaction. He first gave me excuses about the seller being unavailable, then finally divulged that he had received another offer, which the seller was reviewing! While the seller is always free to look at other offers (and the broker is required to present them unless instructed not to do so by the seller), the seller is NOT free to stop performing on a purchase contract he has agreed to unless the buyer defaults or otherwise fails to perform on the contract as agreed. The buyer has rights in the contract, and in fact, can sue the seller for "specific performance" to force the seller to sell him the property on the terms they agreed to if the seller later refuses to complete the transaction.

So now we had a dilemma, one I wanted to resolve. The new offer was allegedly higher than the offer from Big Four Associates (we don't get to verify that, of course), so the seller wasn't quite as happy with the contract he had signed with Big Four Associates. I pressured John to get the seller to show some good faith and paint the building. I also tried to understand how the delay would affect the seller's 1031 exchange, but I wasn't getting any results there...and only unsatisfactory and insufficient response from John. My mentor, Mr. Jim Rohn, would have described himself as being "fascinated" by this new situation!

Bob's Brilliant Idea to Solve The Dilemma

I came up with a brilliant idea! I would call on the seller at his workplace so we could discuss the situation, get to the bottom of the problems, and hopefully arrive at a solution. After all, I knew him personally.

I proceeded to make an appointment with the seller—wearing my electronic sales representative hat—which I was able to set up fairly easily, and I took the seller out for lunch! Of course, I'd come to see the seller as the "electronics sales representative," and we discussed some legitimate business possibilities between supplier and manufacturer, before the conversation shifted to the six-unit apartment building.

The seller had a "better offer" from a backup buyer, but he was not totally sure this new buyer could perform, and of course, he did not want to lose my buyers, if the backup buyer could not perform. I appreciated his dilemma, but he couldn't have both the higher price AND the surety of closing that Big Four Associates brought. Moreover, the buyers were getting antsy, and I could not guarantee that they wouldn't withdraw their offer if the seller didn't perform. Their loan was approved and ready to fund, all inspections were done and their "due diligence" contingencies had been removed. The only thing remaining was for the building to be painted prior to close of escrow.

The Seller Decides on Big Four Associates

The seller decided to honor his contract with Big Four Associates and agreed to schedule the painting ASAP. It appeared that we had salvaged the deal and all was well with this transaction! Awesome!

There was just one small problem I had overlooked. When the seller told broker John about our meeting and its resolution, John was FURIOUS... with ME! In fact, he threatened to fire me before I was able to close my first transaction! I soon learned that my solution to the transaction problem had actually created a bigger problem!

My Brilliant Solution Was Flawed

It turns out that I violated the most sacred protocol between professional real estate agents by blithely contacting JOHN's client directly without John's permission, and I unwittingly exposed our brokerage to a possible lawsuit from the seller, who may or may not be aware of the exact nature of the relationship between the principals and their respective agents. In this particular transaction, our brokerage was acting as a dual agent by representing BOTH the seller and the buyer. It could certainly be construed that my meeting directly with the seller was NOT in his best interests BECAUSE the reason a buyer or seller hires an agent to begin with is to ensure that they are isolated from everyone except their own agent, if and as they so choose.

In fact, had I worked for a different brokerage and approached John's client directly, he would have certainly contacted my broker to complain about my inappropriate conduct. But because I worked for John as an agent of his firm, it was John's problem to wrestle with. Ultimately he discussed the tradeoffs between buyers with the seller, and they agreed that completing the contract with Big Four Associates provided the best and surest outcome and allowed him to complete his 1031 exchange as planned.

The Transaction Is Salvaged and I Am a Lucky Man!

Fortunately for me, John did NOT fire me, and we closed the transaction as agreed with no further complications. I DID apologize to the seller, of course, and assured him that my intent was to facilitate reaching the best outcome for him and the buyers. While the seller was in no way offended,

I narrowly escaped having a very short real estate career, and I learned a key lesson about agency and client relationships!

We always want to get the lesson when we make a mistake. I was very fortunate not to be disciplined by the Department of Real Estate or the local real estate board office for my transgression, which could have cost me my license, and with it, ended my real estate career before it ever began! Even though I intended the seller no harm, and I believe none came to him because of my actions, I definitely failed to observe the boundaries of agent protocol.

Luckily for me, that incident took place some 38 years ago. I was indeed very fortunate that I survived it and lived to learn many more lessons in my long and rewarding real estate brokerage career!

I've included this story to illustrate that all of us, including me, must serve our apprenticeship while we're learning the rules of how business is conducted. While those rules will be different in every discipline and environment, the best way to persevere in learning your new trade is to select an opportunity to associate with high-quality individuals who have learned the lessons you want to learn and who are willing to coach and mentor you about both the fundamentals and the subtleties that you'll need to learn to become good at the job.

There is no shortcut to getting good at the job. It necessarily entails serving your apprenticeship, so be prepared. You WILL make mistakes... and those mistakes will serve to help you learn that you can make errors. As long as you get the lessons, you will survive and continue to improve your skills as you work your way to success. It is the way of the world!

In Chapters Nine and Ten, which focus on how to become a uniquely successful real estate agent, we will skip well past apprenticeship to share some of the techniques and ideas that will help you perform well as a professional investment property specialist as you learn to increase your business and enhance your image and reputation with investors.

There Is Another HUGE Lesson in Real Estate Investing Illustrated Here in Chapter Two:

"Time and inflation are NOT your enemy as a real estate investor!"

Suppose YOU had been the investor who decided to purchase this six-plex in 1980, and it became the first investment property in your portfolio. Today you could still own it free and clear, and the combination of time and inflation would have caused the rents to have risen from $200 per month per unit to at least $1800 per month per unit, thereby increasing the gross annual income to $129,600 (which is 1.2 times what you paid for the entire building in 1980)!

Let's assume that the operating expenses are still about 30% of the property's current income, but the mortgage has been paid off years ago. This property is now what is often called a "cash cow" and produces a net cash flow of approximately 70% after expenses or some $90,720 per year. While we can't be sure what the property would sell for in today's market, a review of comparable properties listed for sale in the area indicates a market value of about $400,000 per rental unit or $2,400,000 total.

So, let's recount what happened:

1. YOU were the buyer, and you initially spent $35,613 to acquire the property.
2. You continued to receive (positive) cash flow throughout your ownership period.
3. The six units are now delivering $90,720 per year in cash flow, and their market value is about $2,400,000, which is your free-and-clear equity.
4. How many similar properties do you wish you had bought over that same period?

The reason we build a portfolio of such properties is to have our money working for us to produce the lifestyle we prefer, and to allow us to have that income from our properties as long as we choose to own them whether we continue to work or not!

There are many other valuable lessons to learn about building your real estate empire, and in Chapter Three, we examine understanding investment properties in more detail.

CHAPTER THREE

Understanding Investment Properties

ATTENTION: Real Estate Agents Considering Becoming Investment Property Specialists (IPSs):

This chapter of *BE IN THE TOP 1%* was written to help real estate investors formulate a plan to achieve or improve their success in the investment property niche, which offers very lucrative rewards to those who understand how to proceed. If you choose to specialize in serving real estate investors, you too need to understand how to proceed as both an investor yourself and as an agent who also understands the investment property marketplace and exactly how to provide exemplary service to the investor clients you serve.

For you to become an exceptional IPS, you need to learn to think like an investor, to understand exactly what investors need, and then to increase and apply your skills to help those investors become more successful while you help yourself become a more adept investor at the same time.

One needs a good sense of humor to appreciate the irony of becoming an IPS so that you can assist investors with their income property transactions, because, up to this point, they have been forced to "fend for themselves." Virtually NO ONE has been available to help them search for performing properties, to help them strategize about making offers, to understand the specifics of the local marketplace, or to assist in analyzing property performance, taxation, tax-deferred exchanges and exit strategies, etc.

The only advantage that has accrued for investors as a result of having had NO HELP from the agent community, is that the investors have been FORCED to become better at finding most of what they needed on their own! Don't be too surprised, therefore, if you find two groups of investors. The first group won't find your offer of help irresistible, because they can do a lot of the work themselves; the second, larger group will eagerly greet you, quickly admitting they still sorely need your assistance in the investment arena.

Here is what we tell those investors about planning for success.

Successful Real Estate Investing

I have been investing in real estate throughout the last seven decades, and I have been pretty successful in acquiring properties that have appreciated and performed well over that time.

But it's mind-boggling to think of how much better I could have done with better coaching, pertinent education, and an earlier realization that investing success is directly proportional to one's ability and willingness to take action when opportunity is in front of you.

If you are not educated, however, you probably will not see the opportunity. But even if you do see it—and you take action before you are prepared—you'll likely become an unguided missile that will surely crash and burn! So how do you strike a balance between education and action?

Plan of Action

What do you need to learn in order to maximize your chances of becoming a successful real estate investor? If you are currently an investor or a would-be investor who wants to become successful at this game, it's imperative that you put together a plan of action that addresses the key reasons WHY you choose to devote your time and energy to this pursuit, as well as HOW you expect to identify and accomplish your investment goals.

Consider these questions:

1. **WHY real estate?**
    - It is arguably the best vehicle for serious, smaller investors. But, why did you choose to follow this path to wealth and independence?
2. **WHAT do you want your real estate investments to do for you?**
    - Provide cash flow to supplement your other income?
    - Supplement or provide all of your retirement income?

- What is a realistic timetable to acquire the necessary portfolio of properties to accomplish those results?
- What is your long-term investment plan?
- What is your exit strategy?

3. **WHO is going to do the research, market studies, and other due diligence necessary to find, analyze, inspect, and prepare offers and negotiate for the properties you wish to acquire?**
   - Once acquired, WHO will manage the properties?
   - Do you have the time, ability, and inclination to do these tasks? Or do you need help?
   - Will you hire assistants or perhaps take on partners?
4. **WHAT resources do you have to work with?**
   - Do you have cash or other liquid assets with which to purchase the properties?
   - Do you have good credit to help you obtain loans to finance the properties?
   - Do you have other collateral or assets you can utilize to obtain credit?
   - Do you have family or other team members with appropriate experience, skills, cash to assist you?

Write it Down

A written plan will help you focus on what you want to accomplish, including the scope of your activities, a preliminary timetable for both the education, planning, and preparation phases, and for acquiring and operating your rental properties as you build your portfolio. A written plan avoids ambiguity and provides an easy way to measure your results. It need not be cast in concrete, of course, because virtually ALL plans require adjustments as we compare what we expected with the results we actually obtained. The process of PLAN, DO, REVIEW allows us to refine our guesstimates, so that we get better and more realistic as we learn the lessons of experience.

Partnering

If you plan to solicit partners or other investors to help you with financing or management of any of your acquisitions, a written plan will help you demonstrate that you've studied the opportunity and the marketplace, and that you understand the tasks to be undertaken. If you expect me—or another investor—to contribute to your project, you'll do well to explain it in sufficient detail for me to decide whether your project merits my attention and interest. Your written plan will give me an opportunity to see how well you've done your homework and whether your invitation to participate is compelling.

We will revisit the concept and importance of partnering with other investors to accelerate your investment results in considerable detail in Chapter Seven: Should Your Investment Strategy Include Taking On Partners? While it's entirely possible for you to succeed without partners, it will be slower and more difficult to achieve ownership of larger properties on your own. We will examine the tradeoffs involved with partnerships versus working alone to achieve your desired results. We will consider how partnerships can be structured to obtain the maximum benefits of cooperative efforts with partners while minimizing the liabilities attendant to partnerships.

Whether you involve partners or not, your written plan should answer the key questions of WHO, WHAT, WHERE, WHEN, WHY, and HOW; should enumerate all resources required; and specify what action is required to amass and incorporate those resources. Be clear about WHO will bring WHAT to the project, and at what cost. Financial strategist Russell Gray[2] says, "Do the math, and the math will tell you what to do." Your plan will help you determine if the project is indeed feasible and worth pursuing.

Getting Educated

Fortunately, there are a lot of available resources to help you get educated about owning and operating investment properties. Classes are available online, at community colleges, at private seminars, and in many books that have been written on the subject of real estate investing. We've included in this book a list of several books and authors whose work provides helpful insights and advice about the basics of investing. Most of these books are inexpensive, but they contain lots of useful ideas and information that you can utilize to improve your knowledge of the methods and techniques available to help you learn the essentials as well as the nuances of the business.

[2] Russell Gray is the co-author of *Equity Happens—Building Lifelong Wealth With Real Estate*

It's also important that you discover the investment community forums where you can interface with other investors, to learn what they are doing, and specifically, to understand what is working for them. There are many ways to pursue an investment career, so ideally, you will progress much more quickly if you are able to compare ideas, techniques, and results with other investors. Many communities have organized real estate investment clubs where you can meet other investors as well as local real estate agents and other professionals who may become valuable team members and advisors to you. If you are a new or blossoming IPS, networking with other agents, investors, and potential team members is one of the best ways you can spend your time.

Your job—as the president of your own real estate investment company—is to learn how to utilize the efforts of your team rather than do every job yourself. That is, you need to be the strategist, not the broker, the lender, the accountant, the painter, or the attorney.

Attending seminars and conferences that include timely information and ideas about investing is what we could call "sharpening our ax." Not only will you hear from professional speakers about topics that affect your daily business, you will have the opportunity to interface and network with other attendees and practitioners who can be great sources of information and occasionally be candidates for your business directly. If you are competing for your client's attention and interest in the investment opportunities, such as syndications you structure and manage, you will be well served by learning everything you can about your competition's investment offerings.

So, make it your goal to learn everything useful to you that you can! You simply cannot know too much, and it is an ever-changing platform. New techniques, new tax rules, new economic situations, and new opportunities will require new methodology for responding and coping with the impact of the changes you encounter. Just be certain to use appropriate professionals to do any jobs that come up and provide the expertise that is required. Don't become a professional inspector when you can hire one instead and depend upon their expertise as a full-time practitioner. Should you choose to invest in multiple marketplaces, you will need local team members at each property location.

The key to becoming a successful investor is to become an educated investor. As you become more competent you also become more confident, which will allow and encourage you to take action and start building your property portfolio. Nothing happens until you take action, so don't wait until you know EVERYTHING you'll ever need to know to get started. When you are comfortable with the process of finding and evaluating properties, understand your strategy, and have the necessary assets in place, it's time to get started. The Real Estate Guys™ motto is "Education for Effective Action." Until you take action, nothing happens. Professional investor Robert Helms asks this question: "How much will you make from real estate you don't own?"

As a new IPS attending meetings with investors, you'll probably be surprised to find that few, if any, other real estate agents will show up. If there are other agents there, make a point of getting to know them too, because there is a good chance they could become part of your private network of IPSs who know the marketplace and will work with you to help sell each other's listings. Knowledgeable IPS agents are definitely a rare breed worth cultivating, and it will be to your advantage to figure out how you can add value to them.

▶ NOTE

One of the best resources I know for real estate investors is The Real Estate Guys™ radio show, which is broadcast weekly, and can be instantly downloaded from their website at www.RealEstateGuysRadio.com every week. Downloading is free, and the program is crammed with current, pertinent information about real estate investment markets worldwide. These podcasts are heard in over 190 countries, by many thousands of listeners weekly, and it is typically one of the top rated real estate program available on iTunes. Don't miss Robert Helms and Russell Gray's incisive commentary and interviews with top authors, writers, speakers, and teachers including the "who's who" of prominent real estate and financial experts.

The Real Estate Guys™ also offer several seminars for investors covering topics such as The Secrets of Successful Syndication, How to Win Funds And Influence People. Go to their website at www.RealEstateGuysRadio.com and click on the EVENTS button for scheduled times and locations.

Personal Investment Philosophy

Robert Helms and Russell Gray, better known as The Real Estate Guys™ and the authors of their book for investors, *Equity Happens*, think it's imperative that you develop your own personal investment philosophy before you start buying properties. This is such an important concept, which most people learn the hard way after realizing that they wish they hadn't been quite so eager to get into contract on properties that actually don't perform too well or perhaps no longer match their investment strategy. Let's examine why this happens all too often.

Usually, we simply haven't taken the time to strategize about what will work best for each of us. That is, we have NO investment strategy!

No two investors are exactly alike; we all have different experiences and attitudes, different educational backgrounds, different financial resources, and different risk tolerances. Until we have clearly identified our strategy—our personal investment philosophy—it's hard to act decisively when the right property is in front of you. Until you know whether you will invest in:

- Condominiums
- Townhomes
- Single-Family Homes
- Duplexes/Triplexes/Fourplexes
- Small Apartment Buildings (5+ Units)
- Mobile Home Parks
- Assisted Living Facilities
- Public Storage Facilities
- Commercial Properties
- New Development Projects (with higher risks, and higher rewards possible)

And...whether you will do it alone or with partners,

And...whether the properties will be located three blocks from your home,

Or...whether they will be located three states away from your home,

Or...whether they will be located in another country,

you're really not quite ready to begin.... You must first invest the time and energy necessary to figure out how—and where—you want to start. Identify the property type(s), the locations, etc., before you plunge into the fray. You'll be glad you did!

Building Your Portfolio of Investment Properties

There are some important preliminary steps you need to take before you write your first offer, so let's consider how to approach these tasks:

1. Selecting the property you want to purchase is literally the LAST step! WHAT?

Yes, it's true! Most of us think we should start by finding a property. We're fired up and ready to go, and we spot that property for sale around the corner. We call the agent, and we make an offer, and we win the bid, and we're on our way! Hooray!

But aren't we just a little ahead of ourselves, here? To really maximize our chances of success, we must first settle on our personal investment philosophy. Then...

2. We must select the marketplace where we wish to begin. For example, you may think that Appaloosa, Kentucky sounds good with its four-year college, medical school, and state prison, but will it support your new rental property with adequate tenant occupancy and cash flow? A thorough analysis of the Appaloosa marketplace is essential before investing there. A "great buy" on a property in Appaloosa isn't necessarily a good enough reason to proceed.

3. We must also select a team of professionals—in Appaloosa or wherever—to help us find, analyze, inspect, obtain financing, prepare and review the offer, manage the property, assess the after tax benefits, and do the ongoing accounting.

Your team will likely consist of:

- Your Realtor/Agent
- Your Lender/Loan Broker
- Your CPA/Accountant/Tax Attorney
- Your Real Estate Attorney

- Your Insurance Agent
- Your Property-Home Inspector
- Your Termite-Pest Inspector
- A Qualified Intermediary to guide your 1031 tax-deferred exchanges
- Your Property Manager (yes, it could be you)
- Other Inspectors as Necessary (Soils Engineer, Foundation Expert, Roofer)

▶ NOTE

IDEALLY, EVERY MEMBER OF YOUR TEAM IS ALSO AN INVESTOR TOO! Being investors themselves will prepare them best for understanding what you're doing and will give them applicable experience to bring to the table.

Additionally, the transaction will utilize the services of title or escrow companies or real estate attorneys to "close" the escrow and may involve homeowner associations and management service companies, etc.

It is common to have 10 to 20 independent service providers involved in your transaction, so be patient, be thorough, and do your homework!

To review, the steps in the purchase process are:

- Determine your personal investment philosophy and decide which type of property you want to purchase.
- Analyze the marketplace FIRST.

If it doesn't look strong enough to predict a successful outcome, LOOK ELSEWHERE!

If it does look strong enough, THEN AND ONLY THEN are you ready to put your team to work in this marketplace!

- Select your team and put them to work. When they have found appropriate candidate properties, ANALYZE the specific performance of each and select the best for your purpose, then submit your bid.

▶ **NOTE**

Unless you're prepared to buy MULTIPLE properties, don't submit multiple offers simultaneously. You may be the winner/winner, and you'll make enemies if you can't perform and probably lose your earnest money deposit too!

We will examine how to go about building your portfolio of investment properties in more detail in Chapter Six.

Analyzing Marketplaces

What essential elements must a marketplace contain to demonstrate the ability to safely support the rental properties you want to buy? In a nutshell, there must be a *continuing* rental demand for the property, at rental rates that allow you to maintain positive after tax cash flow.

Analyzing marketplaces is NOT a simple topic to understand, but it's the key to acquiring real estate that will *perform for you over time.*

The question is, "Does Appaloosa contain a sufficient variety and quantity of industries, businesses, jobs, and employment opportunities to consistently provide sufficient tenants (occupancy) to keep your unit(s) rented at rates that produce adequate positive cash flow for the foreseeable future?"

You must be convinced that it does before you pick the best property you can find in Appaloosa and write your offers.

Property Management

When Do You Need to Hire a Professional Property Manager?

Whether your client is a brand-new, first-time investment property owner or they own and operate 100 or more rental units, the most important factors that will determine their financial success are exactly the same. Namely, they must operate their rental properties with the *highest occupancy rate possible*, and they must *minimize the "turn-over"* occasioned by their present tenants moving out and their needing to replace them with the least "downtime" between tenants.

In short, they need to maximize the income stream the property generates in order to create the optimum cash flow, which determines their profit margin and directly affects the market value of their property.

So, if the key to success is indeed good property management, the question to be addressed is, "Who is going to manage this property? The investor or a professional property manager (PM)?" Of course, the answer might depend on several factors, including the investor's proximity to the property. The option of self-management surely depends largely on that investor's inclinations, experience, the time they have available to self-manage, and perhaps whether self-management is actually the "highest and best" use of their personal time. Let's examine exactly what's required to successfully manage a property from the standpoint of whether the investors already have (or need to acquire) the skills and resources to do it themselves.

Can I (Should I) Self-Manage my Rental Properties?

First, let's acknowledge that many successful investors earnestly believe that "life is way too short to manage my rentals myself!" Clearly, this group is never going to try to put PMs out of business, and it doesn't matter how much the PM's service costs.

Those investors who feel differently enough about this to entertain the idea of self-management, probably fall into two categories: those who are concerned about the cost factor and those who primarily insist on maintaining control or feel they can do the job as well—or better—than the PM.

Rental Housing Associations

Most larger cities around the country have active rental housing associations available to assist property owners in understanding and complying with tenant-landlord laws and regulations. Fees to belong to these associations are generally modest, and they provide significant assistance to landlords, especially in the areas of understanding state and local housing regulations, legal advice, monthly newsletters, seminars, training classes, and events for their members. They also provide "current" rental forms to help ensure compliance with regulations. Whether you manage your properties yourself or employ a professional PM, consider the benefits of joining a rental housing association, if available.

First of all, you will need to understand enough about tenant-landlord law in the city and state where the property is located to help you decide whether to manage the property yourself or to hire a property manager. Rental housing is a regulated industry, and it's imperative that landlords understand both the tenant's and their own rights and responsibilities to avoid unwanted interference by government rental (tenant advocacy) agencies. Remember, your tenant IS your customer, and he or she must be treated with respect. We want HAPPY tenants who will stay with us long-term, pay the rent as agreed (ideally on time), and help us pay for the operation of the property. This is just good business; happy tenants make for happy landlords!

Each and every state in America has its own set of regulations with respect to fair-housing laws, all of which are intended to give the tenant a "fair shake" in the rental marketplace. Some states, like California and New York, are thought of as "tenant friendly" states because the tenant's rights are much stronger, and many of the courts and bureaus will heavily favor the tenant in the event of disputes. Moreover, many cities and municipalities in those "tenant friendly" states have enacted some form of rent control legislation to ensure that the tenants are not victimized by unscrupulous landlords. The net result of such ordinances is that the landlord's net cost to operate rental properties controlled by these ordinances can skyrocket, and the property's value will be diminished accordingly. Some of these well-meaning, but terribly written, ordinances are VERY restrictive, and they can easily place undue burdens on the financial feasibility of operating your property profitably.

Your responsibility as the landlord's agent and as the local investment property specialist is to be sure YOU understand whether rent control is an issue in your town. If there ARE rent control ordinances in place, it's imperative that you research and understand them thoroughly so you can discuss them with your clients and perhaps help them select areas with fewer or no such restrictions. Local rental housing associations and property managers will be intimately familiar with the detailed regulations of rent control ordinances. Ask the housing association or PMs whether there are any classes or seminars conducted locally to help understand the regulations imposed by rent control or other applicable housing rules that must be observed.

Although I prefer to avoid areas with *any* type of rent control altogether, we do now and have previously operated properties in areas with rent control ordinances, and many of them are easy to live with it. However, the more prohibitive ordinances that limit how and when you can change tenants or when you can increase your rents definitely affect the market value of your properties and may simply not be worth the effort they require to comply with the regulations. With respect to rent control, finding the proper political climate is definitely more urgent than finding the best weather conditions for your rental properties.

Hopefully, rent control won't be an issue in your town, but if it is, be sure you know exactly where you can safely operate rental properties successfully.

▶ NOTE

Because there are almost NO such restrictions on commercial properties, (where personal housing is not involved) some investors prefer to concentrate in that arena and avoid dealing with residential tenants altogether. There are no rent control ordinances governing retail, office, industrial, or public storage.

What Does Professional Property Management Cost?

What are the economic considerations of self-management versus professional management of a property? Most property managers charge for their services on either a fixed fee basis or as a percentage of the rents actually collected. Rates vary with the type of property, size of the building(s), scope of management duties, property location and size, and property management company you hire. While the fees charged are important, they are actually NOT the most important factor in selecting a property manager. As with ALL service providers, the nature and quality of the service rendered is usually a function of fees charged. It's far more important to have the exact services you need than to save a few dollars by using the cheapest manager you can find. (A Brian Tracy quote springs to mind: "The pain of poor quality ALWAYS outlasts the pleasure of low price!")

Some management companies divide their fees into two or more categories. They often charge a fee for locating and installing a new tenant if need be, and then charge you on an ongoing basis for administering the property, collecting and disbursing rents, and paying selected bills from your utility companies, repairmen, gardeners, craftsmen, and suppliers. If there are vacancies, the fee to install a new tenant might range from zero to 100% of the first month's rent. If the PM charges a fee to find and install a new tenant, they will typically guarantee the occupancy for six months or so, and if the first tenant doesn't stick, they'll replace them at no cost for a six month period. The PM must advertise, meet, and show the property to the prospective tenants, provide proper rental forms, and accept and screen the tenant's application to rent. It usually entails background checks, calling references, and physically moving the tenant into the unit once they've been approved. At this stage, the PM should review all documents, forms, and policies (including security deposit returns and house rules) with the tenant and give them keys plus copies of all documents. They should also inventory the property, having the tenant essentially agree to its condition upon move-in, which can preclude arguments about the unit's condition upon move-out and minimize the possibility of haggling over responsibility for cleaning and repairs required. Photos are the best evidence of the property's condition.

Fees for administration will vary with region and property type and may often be negotiated based upon exactly which services the PM provides. I personally want my PM to do everything required to interface with tenants including collecting all rents, making most of the monthly payments to service providers, handling any needed repairs, and keeping the rental agreements up-to-date using the most current, legal forms available.

After collecting rents and making payments, the PM sets aside an amount to keep on hand for unforeseen repairs, etc. (say $500 per unit) and then disburses the remainder to me along with a monthly summary of each month's activities. For tax purposes, I also receive a year-end summary and an IRS 1099 reported income form each year. Fees are likely to range from 5% to 12% of the rents collected, so part of the landlord's job in interviewing a PM is to discuss rates and services provided and to understand exactly what they are paying for.

I do not know of any place where landlords are required by ordinance or other laws to hire a PM, but contemplating self-managing a rental located three states away suggests to me that hiring a local PM will probably serve you well and will also be cost effective.

Live-In Resident Manager

In California, landlords are required to have a "live-in resident manager" on the premises if the property contains 16 residential units or more. In that case, either the landlord or his PM will want to supervise this resident manager's daily activities to ensure that the resident manager (RM) understands how to interface with your tenants and what rules of conduct are needed to keep the tenants happy, comply with the law, and keep you out of trouble with housing agencies. This residency requirement has nothing to do with rent control; it applies to all rental properties with 16 or more units in California. The RM is not required to be licensed, but either the professional PM, or the landlord, will need to supervise the RM's activities.

Several other states, counties, and cities require live-in resident managers for multi-unit rental properties, so be sure that you investigate the requirements for areas in which your client intends to operate rental units. Local PMs and housing associations will be very familiar with the local area requirements.

Ironically, although California law requires a live-in resident manager for rentals with 16 units or more, what do you suppose that manager's prescribed duties are? Well, those duties are not clearly defined anywhere to the best of my knowledge! So who decides what the resident manager's duties should be? It would seem likely that the RM would probably be expected to show the units to prospective tenants and then sign rental agreements on behalf of the owner, collect rent monies, issue receipts and keys, explain house rules, check out the vacuum cleaner, assign parking places, handle requests for repairs, post notices, etc.

Clearly, someone needs to perform those functions. Is it the resident manager? Well, it is unclear who does those jobs, so the burden falls upon the building's owner or landlord to create a working plan for the property. If the landlord manages the property himself, then he must also make the determination of the resident manager's duties and how the RM is to be compensated for performing them.

Should those duties be clearly delineated in writing? Oh yes! We cannot expect any employee to do what we ask if it is not PERFECTLY clear what the job entails. Is this an overwhelming task? Not necessarily, but it's one that your owner/landlord may not have planned on having to do, so I suggest it becomes the IPS agent's responsibility to make sure the owner/landlord IS prepared for the task. If you do have a professional PM managing the property, your resident manager's duties may be entirely defined by the PM, whom I would expect to supervise the RM's work. Frankly, it would be a good idea for whomever supervises the RM to provide a written set of instructions or a procedures manual to make sure there are no ambiguities about the RM's duties or to whom he reports.

If an RM is required in your town, make sure your client has made allowances for the cost of having this employee. An RM will typically expect to be given an apartment to live in (or at least a discounted rental rate), and perhaps a salary as well. The landlord will be responsible for the RM's workman's compensation insurance and probably for withholding of state and federal income taxes if there are wages paid. A California live-in RM is considered an employee, and very specific rules apply dictating how much the RM can be charged/credited for his apartment and the minimum wage he must be paid for hours worked.[3]

If you hire a PM, they may prefer to have the RM as one of their employees, so the PM will have supervisorial duties and management responsibilities for the RM, although the landlord will still furnish the RM's personal rental unit. Either way, the cost of having a mandatory RM impacts the landlord's bottom line, so it must be accounted for when calculating your monthly cash flow performance.

In my experience, whether I'm required by law to hire an RM or not, I have found that having someone on site to be my eyes and ears is advantageous—especially if the property is located outside my "tire-kicking radius" and I don't have the ability to physically inspect it occasionally. I always like to designate one of my tenants in a property to let me know how things are going and whether attention is needed. Sometimes, I give them a $50 - $100 per month discount on their rent for tasks like pushing

[3] Compensation for all resident managers in California is subject to the Industrial Welfare Commission's order 11050, see *Order Regulating Wages, Hours, and Working Conditions in the Public Housekeeping Industry* at https://www.dir.ca.gov/t8/11050.html.

the garbage container out for collection, which I've decided is a bargain, and which creates some loyalty.

NOTE

If you are required to have a live-in resident manager, you'll need more than just an active role in overseeing the RM's activities. Whether it's you or a PM who supervises the RM, it's imperative that one of you creates a written operating policy manual detailing how all of the RM's duties and tasks are to be performed. This manual ensures that your RM knows the rules and guidelines for performing the job correctly and will provide the documentation of that should you be sued by a tenant, a tenant's advocacy group, or even the RM himself!

(Yes, the RM must read it and sign an acknowledgment that he has done so!)

No question about it, your life as a landlord will definitely be simpler if you choose your portfolio properties in cities and states that (1) Don't require you to have resident managers and (2) Do not impose any form of rent control!

Hiring a Property Manager

So how do you go about finding and hiring a property manager? Assuming your client has decided to engage a professional PM, how do they begin the search for a suitable manager for the property? What skills and attributes are they looking for, and what are the licensing requirements of the PM? First of all, I suggest you recommend that your landlord client is very clear about HOW they want to be communicated with by the PM (telephone, email, fax, orally, or always-in-writing, etc.) to avoid misunderstandings and to obtain the level of comfort they want with respect to being kept abreast of developments or problems encountered with the property.

Although people skills are a plus, I've found some property managers who are very effective, while decidedly crisp and business-like. The PM's knowledge of the business is paramount, and inserting a PM between you and the tenants is often healthy, especially if you are a "softie" who gives the tenant anything he wants whether it's a good business decision or not.

Let's look at the legal qualifications required of a PM. While there are definite variations in each state, in general, a PM must have a real estate broker's license to oversee or operate a PM business. However, not all of his employees are usually required to be licensed. Some states like Nevada additionally require a special certificate to operate a PM business. Because they handle an owner's money, it's a good idea if they (the PM and the brokerage) are both insured and bonded. Ask to see a copy of the broker's license and the insurance and bonding documents up front.

There are any number of ways to find a candidate PM broker, but the best is ALWAYS a direct referral, if possible. If you know someone using a PM's services in the area of interest, ask for a referral and specifically question your contact about what he does or doesn't like about them. If there is an existing PM other than the present owner, ask about the owner's satisfaction with that manager and talk to the PM as part of your due diligence process. Questioning the PM and, if possible, the tenants is a great source of information. Advise your clients to be careful about approaching the tenants until they are IN CONTRACT. Neither the owner nor your client wants to "spook" the tenants or interfere with their right to privacy. (This is one of the reasons why most income properties are sold "Subject to Inspection.")

As an IPS real estate agent, it will behoove you to become familiar with the active PMs in your area and be prepared to refer them to your clients. PMs can help educate you and your clients about the realities and tradeoffs between candidate properties you are considering purchasing in their area of operations.

You can also consult newspaper ads, rental magazines, local housing and apartment associations, or organizations such as NARPM (National Association of Residential Property Managers at http://www.narpm.org/) to see who is doing business in the area, and then make an appointment to go to the broker's office to see how he runs his shop. Ask whether he or she has written manuals or policies for your review (not imperative) and ask for a representative (sample) copy of the rental agreements and applications they use for tenants and a copy of the employment contract they will use with your client. You'll want to know their rates, whether they're paid based on rents collected or on a flat fee basis, their termination policy, and notice periods required to cancel the contract.

Carefully review the terms of the proffered employment contract between your client and the PM. You may want to have your or your client's real estate attorney look at it also. Why? Because most PMs WRITE THEIR OWN contracts to ensure that it says what they want it to say! The terms are often arbitrary and may not be too user-friendly!

For example, some PM contracts require you to pay a minimum monthly fee whether the unit is rented or not! I personally don't like this approach because I feel it disincentivizes them, i.e., what's the rush to get your unit rented if the PM is getting paid either way? Many will stipulate that the agreement is in effect for one year with automatic yearly renewal and a that a notice is required to terminate the contract. This works for me, provided I can give notice to terminate in 30 days AT-ANY-TIME without cause.

Every employment contract should be negotiable. If you cannot arrive at suitable terms, it's time to move on and look at other candidate PMs!

And of course, you want a list of the PMs current and past clients that you can contact for input. Here are some questions to ask the PM that will help you determine their suitability for your project:

- What type of units, and approximately how many units, do you currently manage?
- Are you a sole proprietor or do you have associates that assist you with property management?
  - If so, are they regularly compelled to attend industry seminars, conferences, and training sessions?
  - Do they handle rent money, and if so, are they individually bonded?
  - Do you provide workman's compensation insurance for them?
- Do you carry E and O insurance?
- Tell me about the current market for the units my clients are buying.
- What are vacancy rates in this area?
- What are the trends?
- Are you experiencing any particular problems we should be aware of?

- Is there any form of rent control here?
- What additional resources, if any, will you need to get the job done?
- Are you an investor yourself?
- Where do you own rental properties?
- If you do not, why not? (Just as we prefer realtors that own and specialize in rental properties, it's desirable to have a PM with the same mentality and personal experience, whenever possible.)
- Who do you use for repairs? Your own staff? Or if not, how do you select repairmen? (Most NARPM chapters and apartment associations have a cadre of affiliate members who provide repairs and services for the PMs.)
- What is your policy about returning phone calls (from both the owner and the tenants?), e.g. "within 24 hours," "when you get around to it?"
- Do you have an on-call person after hours and on weekends?

▶ NOTE

Poor habits about returning calls is the major complaint of owners who are looking to replace their current PMs!

- Are you a member of any apartment associations that provide you with legal guidance, legislation updates, currently-approved rental forms and notices? Should I or the landlord also become a member?

▶ NOTE

Whether it is a residential or a commercial property, it's important to determine if there is a homeowner's association involved, and if so, to review and understand the rules and regulations of the association, especially what powers they have in controlling the association members and properties.

What's the Next Step?

If you're comfortable with your overall understanding of the marketplace and are ready to go, then get your financing in order and get busy making offers so that you can put that knowledge to work and start reaping the benefits of owning investment property. If appropriate, hire a property manager and pay close attention to how the relationship goes so that you can comfortably entrust the management to them and you can get on with your life!

Do not let problems (and there will be problems when you're dealing with tenants) dissuade you from operating your rental properties successfully.

This will all seem easier once you have some experience under your belt, and you'll be ready to expand your real estate empire! Good luck and much success to you in operating your rental properties!

Recommended Reading List

1. *Equity Happens* by Robert Helms and Russell Gray
2. *Rich Dad, Poor Dad* by Robert Kiyosaki
3. *How to Master the Art of Selling* by Tom Hopkins
4. *The ABC's of Real Estate Investing* by Ken McElroy
5. *Before You Quit Your Job* by Robert Kiyosaki
6. *Rich Woman* by Kim Kiyosaki
7. *Why We Want You To Be Rich* by Robert Kiyosaki & Donald Trump
8. *The Sleeping Giant (The Awakening of the Self-Employed Entrepreneur)* by Ken McElroy
9. *Own Your Own Corporation* by Garrett Sutton

CHAPTER FOUR

Valuing Investment Properties

Real estate investing is a business and, like any business, must be operated profitably to continue to exist. Becoming a successful real estate investor means you must acquire a thorough understanding of the operation and management of the real estate properties you buy, sell, and operate whether you are a long-term buy-and-hold investor or a short-term flipper.

Those who flip properties typically buy them in distressed or obsolete condition then spend time and money adding improvements that will increase their market value in terms of both monthly rental income and the price buyers are willing to pay to acquire them. A lot of buy-and-hold investors start their investing career by flipping properties until they build up enough cash to serve as the down payment to begin acquiring properties for their buy-and-hold portfolio.

These flippers often use what we might call a flip-and-hold strategy. They buy a property, renovate it to produce higher income (therefore higher value), refinance it based on its new cash flow and value (oftentimes receiving all or most of their initial investment back), and then keep that property in their portfolio long-term rather than flip or sell it. This provides the buyer with his funds back to spend on his next renovation, and he keeps an improved property whose return on investment will be at-or-close-to "infinite" because he has little or none of his initial money still invested while he enjoys continuing cash flow.

Some beginning would-be investors don't have sufficient funds to buy and close on the property or complete the necessary repairs and improvements, so they spend their time chasing and bidding on properties. These folks are called wholesalers, because they normally sell their position in any property on which they are the winning bidder to a flipper who pays them a fee for having secured the property.

To be sure, some wholesalers are quite substantial and have created significant businesses in the single-family rental and smaller multifamily segments of the rental housing market. Larger wholesalers may include real estate brokerage in their offerings, focusing on finding inventory for investors and also handling resale homes for first-time buyers.

These wholesalers and flippers are not considered to be investors by the IRS until they acquire properties that are "either used in a trade or business or held for the production of income," with the intention of making a profit over the time they own these properties. If you are not "holding your properties for the production of income," and are turning them (however long that takes), without having rented them to a tenant, you are considered to be a "dealer," and the profits made by dealers are taxed as ordinary income.

Becoming a Long-Term Buy-And-Hold Investor

Although it's not absolutely necessary to become a buy-and-hold investor, this is the path taken by most successful, long-term investors. If you treat your real estate investment business like an on-again, off-again hobby, it may not be as important that you put together a plan to provide for your success over the long haul. But most serious investors have determined that their goal in real estate investing is to build a portfolio of income-producing properties that will ultimately provide or supplement their retirement income, and will help them achieve an abundant lifestyle where they no longer need to work for money, but instead, through their investments, have their money working for them…they no longer need a job to provide for the lifestyle they have created for themselves.

When we become long-term investors, we benefit from the tax breaks regularly available to investors, which significantly enhances our ability to operate our rental properties profitably, and helps us continue to grow equity in them over time.

▶ **NOTE**

We will examine the many tax benefits allowed for real estate investors in greater detail in Chapter Five: Tax Benefits of Owning Real Estate

---

So if our goal as investors is to make a profit through selling or operating our properties, it's vital that we know how to determine the value of those properties in the marketplace.

If you are a real estate investment property specialist, your job is not only to understand the methods used to value investment properties, but also to be able to assist your investor clients in thoroughly understanding and using these tools when they are buying or selling properties for their portfolio.

"Do the Math and the Math Will Tell You What to Do!"

Before we go any further learning about the mathematics and methods of property evaluation, I realize that some of you may suffer from the same malady Russell Gray of The Real Estate Guys™ grew up with, which he calls "arithmophobia." Russ says he was terrible at math as a student. He hated math and avoided it at all costs until he eventually discovered that it was MUCH easier and ENORMOUSLY more interesting when the numbers were associated with dollar signs! Today, Russ is an acknowledged financial strategist and one of the best self-taught economists I know. Perhaps the quote Russ is most famous for is: "Do the math and the math will tell you what to do!" Yes, the big-time math hater now proclaims that doing the math will give you the solution you are looking for! And, as usual, he's right about that!

So remember, mathematics is just a TOOL which allows us to compare investments, and with practice, even "arithmophobics" can readily understand the concepts used to value investment properties. The math we will use is not really that difficult, so DON'T let it intimidate you! If you find yourself stumbling over the numbers, take time to review WHAT we're calculating, and the method we're utilizing to find the results we're after. If we use the correct method, we'll obtain the correct numbers we're after every time! If Russ can do it, YOU can do it, too! To be sure, we look at much more than math when evaluating a property, but we want to master the math, because it's ALWAYS an essential part of analyzing any property.

Now, let's start the discussion on valuation by considering some specific ways that are commonly used to determine a property's market value.

Production of Income

Both businesses and properties can be valued based upon the income they produce annually. For example, it is common practice for someone buying an operating commercial business to pay the seller a price that is a multiple of the business' gross annual income. A dry-cleaning business might sell for three to four times the gross income it produced last year.

Similarly, an apartment building will sell at some multiple of the gross rental income it generates annually. In fact, what the buyer is buying in both cases is the income stream generated by the business or the property. Since each buyer's precise purpose in investing their capital is to obtain an income stream, their goal is for that income to be sufficient to return them a net profit, after expenses. How much they can or will pay to purchase the income stream depends upon the return on investment they can obtain.

Gross Rent Multiplier

When an apartment building or other income-producing property is listed for sale, one of the parameters we use to determine its performance is the gross rent multiplier or GRM. Remember, we are buying the income stream, so the GRM tells us immediately what we are paying for that property and its income stream in terms of the total annual income it produces. While knowing the GRM is not sufficient information to make an offer to purchase the property, it IS adequate to determine if the property is even a candidate to buy when compared with other listings in this marketplace.

Let's look at an example of how we can use a property's GRM as a screening tool:

At any given time in a particular marketplace, we can inspect or calculate the range of GRMs of the properties we are interested in selling.

If we find a property listed for sale at a GRM of 10, that means the seller is asking 10 times the annual income produced as the selling price for the property. So, for example, if the listed price is $1,000,000 and the annual income is $100,000, the GRM will be 10.

$$\begin{aligned} \text{GRM} &= \text{List Price (or Fair Market Value)} \div \text{Annual Income} \\ &= \$1{,}000{,}000 \div \$100{,}000 \\ &= 10 \end{aligned}$$

Even if the GRM of the property is not shown in the listing data, it is easily calculated, and we can use it to establish how the property is priced compared to similar properties in this marketplace.

If we calculate the individual GRMs of those similar properties using the list price and the annual income of each, we can now compile a list of GRMs for each of the properties we are comparing (See Figure 2). If there are 20 such comparable properties, we can calculate the average GRM by adding the individual GRMs together then dividing by the number of units compared (20 in this case). We now know the average GRM and the range of GRMs for this group of properties. (In this example, 20 similar properties are showing GRMs ranging from 7 to 12 times the annual income produced, and the average GRM is 9.70).

FIGURE 2

Comparison of Gross Rent Multipliers (GRMs) for 20 Similar Properties in a Marketplace

PROPERTY	FMV/LIST PRICE	ANNUAL INCOME	CALCULATED GRM
Property 1	$ 750,000	$ 88,250	8.50
Property 2	$ 795,000	$ 95,400	8.33
Property 3	$ 825,000	$ 90,760	9.09
Property 4	$ 867,500	$ 94,000	9.23
Property 5	$ 895,000	$ 92,560	9.67
Property 6	$ 920,500	$ 99,500	9.25
Property 7	$ 975,000	$118,900	8.20
Property 8	$ 999,750	$ 98,020	10.20
Property 9	$1,115,000	$104,200	10.70
Property 10	$1,250,000	$104,167	12.00
Property 11	$1,350,000	$122,400	11.03
Property 12	$1,350,000	$126,270	10.69
Property 13	$1,399,500	$125,500	11.15
Property 14	$1,455,995	$184,775	7.88
Property 15	$1,500,000	$214,286	7.00
Property 16	$1,565,000	$180,716	8.66
Property 17	$1,575,500	$148,632	10.60
Property 18	$1,675,000	$160,440	10.44
Property 19	$1,690,000	$148,245	11.40
Property 20	$1,700,000	$171,700	9.90
			total: 193.92

To find the average GRM for this group of properties, simply divide the total by the number of properties compared.

In this example, the average **GRM = 193.92 ÷ 20 = 9.70**.

The range of GRMs for these 20 properties is from 7.00 to 12.00.

Since our primary concern is return on our investment, it's clear that the lower the GRM, the less we have to spend to buy the income stream we're after. So, when we calculate the return we can expect, we may also be able to determine approximately how high the "allowable" GRM can be for the property to be a candidate for us to purchase. If our calculations show, for example, that we can only obtain a satisfactory return when the GRM is 9 or less, we can now rule out those properties with GRMs greater than 9 from our list of 20 properties examined. In this example, properties number 1, 2, 7, 14, 15, and 16 would definitely be candidates, and properties number 3, 4, and 6 are close enough to include in your detailed analysis.

▶ NOTE

As a buyer, we are always looking for the lowest GRM we can find. The lower the GRM, the less we pay for the property's income stream.

Calculating Return on Investment

Although a property's GRM is a very useful tool, it is not sufficient data in itself to use to structure an offer to purchase a property. Utilizing the GRM will tell us what the seller is asking as a function of its income, but until we know what it costs to operate the property, we still don't know how much profit will be produced after expenses! Clearly, we need a more detailed analysis of the property's operation. To do that analysis, we utilize what is commonly called the basic income formula, which provides a more detailed look at the property's operation.

Basic Income Formula

We start by determining the gross scheduled income, or GSI. The GSI is the rent that would be collected if all scheduled rents were collected one hundred percent of the time. That seldom happens in real life because of vacancies, turnover, or an inability to actually collect the scheduled rental amount. These unplanned "losses" are attributed to vacancy and bad debt, so at this point our accounting looks like this:

Gross Scheduled Income (GSI)	**$100,000**
– Vacancy and Bad Debt (5%)	**– $ 5,000**
Gross Operating Income	**$ 95,000**

In this example, we now have $95,000 available with which to operate the property for a one year period.

If the operating expenses spent on salaries, maintenance, upgrades, repairs, utilities, property taxes, insurance, legal and accounting services, and property management total 30% of the GSI, we then have:

Gross Scheduled Income	**$100,000**
– Vacancy and Bad Debt (5%)	**– $ 5,000**
Gross Operating Income	**$ 95,000**
– Operating Expenses (30%)	**– $ 30,000**
Net Operating Income	**$ 65,000**

So, we have identified the following items:

The GSI, or gross scheduled income, represents the theoretical maximum rent due.

The GOI, or gross operating income, is what we ACTUALLY collect and have available to operate the property.

The NOI, or net operating income, is what's left after we pay all operating expenses

If we are paying $1,000,000 cash to purchase this property, our resulting income stream (our cash flow) is $65,000 per year. This is more accurately called our before tax cash flow (BTCF), because the tax benefits of ownership have not yet been considered.

If we cannot or choose not to pay cash for the property, we'll need to get a purchase money loan from either a commercial or private lender to complete the purchase. Oftentimes, we can ask the seller to become the lender by carrying back a loan for the property over perhaps a twenty year period. This is particularly attractive to the seller who wants to create an installment sale so that the taxes he pays on the capital gains he's earned on the property are spread out over the twenty year period rather than paid as a lump sum in the year of the sale.

Whatever loan we choose, the annual payments on the loan must now be included in the basic income formula and are entered as debt service (because we are "servicing the debt" as we make principal and interest payments on the loan):

Gross Scheduled Income	**$100,000**
– Vacancy and Bad Debt (5%)	**– $ 5,000**
Gross Operating Income	**$ 95,000**
– Operating Expenses (30%)	**– $ 30,000**
Net Operating Income	**$ 65,000**
– Loan Payments (Debt Service)	**–$ 60,000**
Before Tax Cash Flow (BTCF)	**$ 5,000**

Capitalization Rate

We use the net operating income (NOI) to calculate the capitalization rate, or cap rate, which reflects the property's return on investment after all operating expenses have been included. Because NOI does not take debt service into account, the cap rate is the same whether or not a loan is used to buy the property.

▶ **NOTE**

Net operating income (NOI) reflects the *building's* performance, and it's the same whether the buyer paid all cash, or used a purchase money loan to acquire the property.

Cap rate is calculated by dividing the net operating income by the purchase price or fair market value (FMV) of the property and is expressed as a percentage:

Cap Rate = NOI ÷ Purchase Price or FMV
= $65,000 ÷ $1,000,000
= 6.5%

Many investors use cap rates to target their acquisitions, and appraisers use them to determine fair market values. The range of cap rates acceptable to investors varies widely depending upon their intended use for the properties. As you can see, lower cap rates reflect lower returns on investment, but the amount of the *current* return is less important for properties that will undergo remodeling, etc., in order to increase their rental income, which increases their NOI and, ultimately, their profitability. The acceptability of a current or projected cap rate is definitely in the eye of the beholder!

▶ **NOTE**

As a buyer, we normally look for the highest cap rate we can find. The higher the cap rate, the higher the return on our investment.

So we've learned that both GRMs and cap rates are useful tools in the search for properties we want to add to our portfolio. In general, both provide useful comparative data between competing properties, but cap rates are usually more significant because they take the property's operating expenses into account and therefore reflect the operating return the investor can expect to obtain.

What we really want to know is *everything* about the property that affects its performance, including the likelihood that it will continue to perform well for the period of time we intend to own it. When we discover a candidate property, how do we get our hands on ALL its operating data? What we are after is called an APOD, and it is usually provided to prospective buyers by the listing broker or property owner.

APOD

An APOD is the annual property operating data, and ideally, it provides a detailed breakdown of the property's vital information, including not only its operating parameters, but also a description of the configuration, amenities, number and type of individual rentable units, other sources of income (laundry facility, vending machines, parking fees, etc.), and any unique features of the property. The operating parameters may specify the rental rates and current occupancy of each unit, the amount of security deposits held, the number and cost of employees, if any, and whether a professional property manager (PM) is utilized to manage the property. The more information provided, the better.

▶ **NOTE**

An APOD can be an annual statement of the current operation of the property, but it may instead be a pro forma projection based on whatever assumptions the broker or owner are using to create it. Clearly, it is very important to know what that representation is before you proceed.

The broker who furnishes the APOD in good faith may be totally accurate about the amount of the market rents—but don't bet on it! He won't purposely lie to you, but he might be optimistic or a bit cavalier about what market rents are for the area.

A property manager is generally a much more reliable source for rental rate information because he must *deliver* tenants at the rates he quotes you!

So, don't be nervous about using an APOD; it's a great tool that we want to study whenever it's available for a property we're examining. Just be certain to verify the accuracy of any information you're depending on for your analysis!

What does an APOD look like, and how do we utilize it?

We'll start by reviewing a sample APOD to help us understand what information is normally provided and how we use the APOD to determine the expected before tax cash flow (BTCF). An APOD is designed to help us evaluate a specific property on its own merits, and valuing properties does not normally take the buyer's tax benefits into consideration. We prefer to use an APOD format which DOES include an estimate of the buyers after tax cash flow (ATCF) for each property, so you will see variations in the actual formats preferred by various users.

FIGURE 3

APOD Example – Twenty Units in Austin, Texas

One Bedroom Units in Good Rental Area

$1,295,000   GRM: 10.5   Cap Rate: 5.5%

Cash Flow Analysis

35% Down Payment $453,250

65% New First Loan $841,750

(Debt Service = $5,169 per month principal and interest)

(Loan based on commercial rate of 5.5% per annum, 25 years)

Before Tax Cash Flow

Income:	$10,280 per month
– 30% Expenses:	– $3,084 per month
Net Operating Income:	$7,196 per month
– Debt Service:	– $5,169 per month
Net Spendable Income:	$2,027 per month

After Tax Cash Flow

Assume depreciation at 80%:

($1,295,000 x 0.8) ÷ 27.5 yrs. = $37,673/yr. = $3,139/mo.

At a 37% combined Fed/State tax bracket, this is $1,162/mo.

So, the ATCF is approximately $2,027 + $1,162 = $3,189/mo. = $38,268/yr.

This is an 8.4% cash on cash return on your initial investment.

Generally, the APOD will have room to include the important features of the property you're evaluating, and you can calculate how well it will perform using available or proposed financing options. If the APOD does not contain everything necessary for a satisfactory evaluation, make a list of your questions and ask the broker for the answers you need.

APOD – Twenty Units in Austin Texas

Figure 3 is a completed APOD showing the expected performance of a twenty-unit apartment complex in Austin, Texas, based upon utilizing an available conventional loan to finance the purchase of the units. Let's review the financial analysis and results obtained.

The asking price is $1,295,000. A GRM of 10.5 means the seller has priced the property at 10.5 times its annual income. The cap rate shows a return on investment of 5.5% after paying all expenses.

Another commonly used parameter for comparison to other units in the local marketplace is the price per unit or the price per square foot. In this case we don't know the number of square feet, but we can readily calculate the price per unit as $1,295,000 ÷ 20 units = $64,750 per unit.

Cash Flow Analysis

This performance analysis is based upon using a 25-year, 65% LTV commercial loan in the amount of $841,750, which will require a monthly payment of $5,169, principal and interest at an interest rate of 5.5% per annum.

With commercial loans of the type proposed here, the lender will require that the property produces an income that is greater than the mortgage payment required to debt service the loan by a margin. This margin is known as the debt coverage ratio, or DCR. The lender will establish the DCR they need based upon their assessment of the risk the loan represents to them. DCRs commonly range from values of 1.2 to 1.5, which means that the property they are making the loan on must produce a net operating income (NOI) of at least 1.2 to 1.5 times the payment required to fully service the loan. This 20-unit property's DCR is 1.4 (Net Operating Income ÷ Debt Service).

So, the DCR is the lender's safety factor to allow for the risk that anything may reduce the property's scheduled income or increase its expenses. For example, risks may include:

1. Variation in actual rents collected versus rents projected
2. Variations in market rental rates and occupancy rates over the life of the loan

3. The effect of any other variables the lender deems appropriate.

Before Tax Cash Flow (BTCF)

The monthly income is shown at $10,280. No detail is provided showing whether this gross number includes income from laundry, vending machines, parking, etc. In general, we'd like to know what the income is comprised of to help us compare units and to determine the stability of the income. If we are contemplating upgrading the units to increase income and add value, we'll want to know the details of the current income breakdown and amenities provided.

Expenses are shown at 30% of the gross scheduled income, which is common for this type of building, but some properties will cost more to operate, especially older units. The net spendable income (NSI) before taxes is $2,027 per month, which is $24,324 per year, so the BTCF cash-on-cash return is:

NSI ÷ Down Payment = Cash-on-Cash Return, or

$24,324 ÷ $453,250 = 5.4% of the Buyer's Investment.

▶ **NOTE**

Although the math used is fairly simple, it's essential that you have a financial calculator to calculate loan amortization, balances, and other useful figures. You can find an HP-12C (approximately 3" x 5"x 1/2"size) for $50 to $100 online, or you can install an amortization calculator application on most smart cell phones at low cost.

After Tax Cash Flow (ATCF)

To determine the ATCF, we need to quantify how the benefit of depreciation impacts the buyer's total return on investment.

Calculating the depreciation at 80% means that we are assigning 80% of the property's total value to the "improvements" (buildings, contents, landscaping, etc.), which ARE depreciable, and the remaining 20% to the land itself, which is NOT depreciable. For residential properties, the depreciation period is 27.5 years, while commercial properties are depreciated over a 39 year period. Applying the residential formula in this case yields:

(\$1,295,000 x 0.8) ÷ 27.5 years =
\$1,036,000 ÷ 27.5 years =
\$37,673 per year = \$3,139 per month total depreciation.

If the new buyer has a combined federal/state income tax bracket of 37%, he can utilize 37% of this amount, or \$1,162 per month as a tax deduction. The buyer's ATCF is the combination of his net spendable income and his depreciation deduction, or:

\$2,027 per month + \$1,162 per month =
\$3,189 per month = \$38,268 per year

His after tax cash-on-cash return is now 8.4% of his initial investment.
\$38,268 ÷ \$453,250 = 8.4%

So, the depreciation allowance increased the buyer's BTCF from 5.4%, to an ATCF of 8.4%, an overall cash-on-cash return increase of some 55%, which is an additional ATCF of:

\$38,268 per year - \$24,324 per year = \$13,944 per year return

---

▶ NOTE

The decision to assign 80% of the total property value as depreciable improvements is based upon experience, and your CPA or tax attorney can help you decide whether you should be more "aggressive" about assigning a higher ratio of improvements-to-land for each property you operate. Because this is a multi-story apartment building, it could easily have a major portion of the property's value attributable to improvements, with very little remaining unused land. In that situation, the improvements would contribute a higher portion of the property's total value, so you could justify using an improvement value of greater than 80% to calculate depreciation.

Figure 4 is a blank APOD template that you can use if you so choose. There are many versions of usable APOD templates available from several sources, which may be either more or less complex, or you can design your own. Whatever APOD format you prefer, adopt one of them, because you will be using it repeatedly to analyze properties.

FIGURE 4 - BLANK APOD

APOD

Property Type and Location

PHOTO

OF

PROPERTY

Description of Units/Marketing Emphasis

Price: ________ GRM: ________ Cap Rate: ________

Cash Flow Analysis

___% Down Payment $ ________

___% New First Loan $ ________ (Debt service = $_____/Mo. Principle and Interest)

(Loan based on commercial rate of ___% per annum, ___ years)

Before Tax Cash Flow

Income:	$_________/mo.
– ____% Expenses:	– $_________/mo.
Net Operating Income:	$_________/mo.
– Debt Service	– $_________/mo.
Net Spendable Income:	$_________/mo.

After Tax Cash Flow

Depreciation of ___%: $ ________/yr. = $ ________/mo.

At a ___% combined Fed/State tax bracket, this is $ ________/mo.
So, the ATCF is – $ ________ + $ ________ = $ ________/mo. = $ ________/yr.

This is a ______% cash on cash return on your initial investment.

FIGURE 5

I did not create this figure. I only created the mathematical analysis and discussion of the mythical Mission Oaks Apartments. I would love to give credit due to the author, but despite my research, I remain unaware of this document's origins.

Annual Property Operating Data

Property:	Mission Oaks Apartments		**Price:**	$4,500,000
Location:	2200 W. John Carpenter Freeway, Irvine, TX 75063		**Loans:**	3,300,000
No. Units:	100 **Age:** 1998	**Sq. Footage:** 83,000	**Down:**	1,200,000

	Annual $	% of GOI	$/Unit	Annual $
Gross Scheduled Income				$ 668,400
– Vacancy & Credit Loss @ 5%				33,420
Effective Gross Income				$ 634,980
Laundry Income				12,000
+ Other Income				66,885
Gross Operating Income				$ 713,865
Operating Expenses	**Annual $**	**% of GOI**	**$/Unit**	
Real Estate Taxes	85,000	11.97	850	
Insurance	4,800	0.67	48	
Water/Sewer	13,400	1.88	134	
Trash	16,000	2.24	160	
Property Management	71,387	10.00	714	
Electric	2,200	0.31	22	
Repairs/Maintenance	42,832	6.00	428	
Advertising	4,800	0.67	48	
Telephone	3,200	0.45	32	
Landscaping	2,800	0.39	28	
Miscellaneous	5,580	0.78	56	
Total Operating Expenses	251,998	35.30	2,520	251,998
Net Operating Income				$ 461,867
Proposed Investment				
Down Payment (26.67%)	1,200,000			
+ Acq Costs	45,000			
+ Loan Points	66,000			
Total Investment	1,311,000			
First Loan: $3,150,000, fixed-rate, 6.5%, 30 yrs., 2% pts. (70% LTV)				
Second Loan: $150,000, fixed-rate, 8.5%, 25 yrs., 2% pts.				
LTV: 73.33% DCR: 1.81 BER: 71.07%				
First-year Capital Additions	50,000			
• Loan Scheduled	25,000			
Non-funded Capital Additions	25,000			25,000
Replacement Reserves				30,000
Annual Debt Service				255,354
Cash Flow Before Taxes				$ 151,513

Capitalization Rate	10.26%
Gross Rent Multiplier	6.73
Price Per Unit	$45,000
Price per Square Foot	$54.22
Cash on Cash	11.56%

NOTE: An APOD can reflect either current or projected operation of the property, and is intended to give the analyst a performance evaluation for the first year of operation using these assumptions.

APOD Analysis – Mission Oaks Apartments

Next, we will review the APOD for the Mission Oaks Apartments in Irvine, Texas. The first thing you will notice is that this APOD format includes more detail than the one we just reviewed, but it leaves any ATCF calculations to the potential buyer.

The Mission Oaks Apartments complex is a rather large property, comprised of 100 units, built in 1998. The total building area is 83,000 square feet. No photos are included. The seller is asking $4,500,000 for these units, and it has a high LTV (loan-to-value) loan package available totaling $3,300,000 (73.33% of the purchase price), so the required down payment is $1,200,000, or 26.67%. The proffered loans (a first and second) are attractive 25 and 30 year, fixed-rate loans, at the cost of two points (2%) each.

Before we study the detail in the APOD, note that there is a "snapshot" of the property's performance given at the bottom of the page, which shows five key parameters of interest. The cap rate and GRM have been calculated at 10.26%, and 6.73, respectively, and acquisition cost is shown in terms of both price per unit ($45,000), and its price per square foot ($54.22). The last item is the cash-on-cash return at 11.56%.

It wouldn't be surprising if the seller and his broker arrived at the list price using the $45,000 per unit as a starting point, and then decided that the other performance indicators looked consistent at that price.

In any event, each of these performance indicators allows us to compare this property to other properties in this or other marketplaces. If they weren't included in the data, we would be asking the listing broker for them to help us evaluate the property.

Now, if you turn to the detailed information, you'll note that the APOD gives the basic income formula calculations to show the breakdown of income and expenses. This form uses the term effective gross income to account for vacancy and bad debt losses then adds in income from other sources (laundry, etc.) to arrive at the gross operating income.

Two things are notable in the income portion of the APOD: The first is that the average scheduled monthly rent is $557 per month.

($668,400 ÷ 100 ÷ 12 = $557)

We don't know the size of the units, but this suggests they are probably one bedrooms or large studios. The total square footage of 83,000 square feet divided over 100 units when added to the common and office areas, also indicates that each unit probably averages about 800 square feet of living space.

The second item—which is perhaps of even more interest—states that the complex is also generating a whopping $78,885 per year in "other income," of which about $10 a month per unit is attributable to laundry fees and the balance of $55.74 per month per unit

$$\$66,885 \div 100 \div 12 = \$55.74$$

is obtained from an unspecified source.

Because this is equivalent to an additional 10% a month per unit of income, it has a sizeable impact on the property's performance. It will therefore be important to learn the details about this source of additional income, with particular attention paid to how sustainable it is. It might be rental income for parking or a cell tower, but whatever its source, we'll want to know that information.

As we look at the operating expenses, you will note that they total about 35% of the gross operating income which is typical of this type of property. What isn't necessarily typical, however, is that most of that is being paid for property taxes and property management fees (22%), while all other expenses make up the remaining 13%. Property management (PM) fees vary in different areas, typically running from 5% to 12% of rents collected. This PM cost is at a 10% rate, which may or may not be common in this area. Higher property taxes are common in states that don't collect state income tax fees, but Texas does collect state fees, so these property taxes (about 12%) seem inordinately high.

With the commercial loans of the type proposed here, the lender will require a debt coverage ratio, or DCR, based upon their assessment of the risk the loan represents to them. You'll remember that DCRs commonly range from values of 1.2 to 1.5, meaning that the property they are making the loan on must produce a net operating income of at least 1.2 to 1.5 times the payment required to fully service the loan. This property has a very comfortable margin with a DCR of 1.81.

The final thing to note from the APOD is that the seller or broker is anticipating that a first-year capital addition by the new buyer of $50,000 is planned, which would require the buyer to expend $25,000 cash and acquire a new $25,000 loan. No explanation is offered, so we will want to know exactly what this planned capital addition is for and why it is needed.

So, we have learned quite a lot about this property by this exercise. There are additional questions we need answered before we decide to make an offer on the Mission Oaks Apartments, but we might summarize our findings as follows:

Performance Parameter	**Comments**
GRM	6.73 is definitely workable
Cap Rate	10.26% is definitely workable
New Loans	Attractive; High LTV with low rates create cash-on-cash return of 11.56%
Questions for seller	Source of "other" income? Sustainable? Purpose of $50K capital addition?

Do We Make an Offer?

At this stage, perhaps we haven't learned quite enough to make an offer for the Mission Oaks Apartments, but I think this property looks attractive enough to get our remaining questions answered and to make sure we know the seller's objectives (what else does the seller really want?) so that we can proceed if those questions are answered to our satisfaction. One piece of information not included in the APOD is the total size of the property in acres or square feet. It would be interesting to know if there is enough land to consider adding additional units. We can probably determine that when we inspect the property, before submitting an offer. In any case, it performs well enough that being able to add more units would be a bonus, not a necessity.

Whether there is room to expand or not, I like several things about this property. First of all, the operating parameters are attractive, including the loan package available and the high cash-on-cash returns projected. Moreover, the property appears to be well stabilized and it exhibits good performance. If we decide to pursue it, our job is to verify that these assumptions are correct.

If you are a new investor or a new real estate investment property specialist, don't be overwhelmed by the price and operating costs of the $4,500,000 Mission Oaks Apartments example we've used here in understanding APODs. Purchasing such a property may seem unrealistic at this stage of your career, but most of us want to get to this level, and the principles would be exactly the same if this was a $450,000 property and all the other numbers were also divided by 10.

Caveat Emptor – Let the Buyer Beware

Be advised that there is very little "due diligence" required by law or statute that a buyer must perform before purchasing a property, but it should be clear that the burden of discovery to determine the suitability of any item or property purchased rests with the buyer himself. Short of concealment of damages or fraud, there is probably little recourse to the seller once your transaction has closed. So, it is YOUR job to do your homework and examine all the things that are important enough to affect the property's performance before you complete the purchase. But make no mistake, you will never make a dime on property you don't own, so get prepared to take action! Don't be afraid to complete your property evaluation, make an offer, and proceed to start building your portfolio of properties!

Review of Valuation Terms

Before we leave this discussion of valuing investment properties, let's quickly review the terms and concepts used, because we will be using them routinely as we learn to analyze the strengths and weaknesses of properties we and our investors want to buy, sell, or exchange.

Gross Rent Multiplier or GRM: This number immediately tells us the relationship between the income the property produces annually and its listed price or fair market value. For example, a GRM of 9.5 reflects a listed price or fair market value that is 9.5 times the annual income it produces.

Basic Income Formula: Unlike the GRM—which doesn't take into account the profitability of the property—the basic income formula allows us to calculate return on investment AFTER expenses have been paid, giving us a method to compare the relative performance of several properties in terms of the cash-on-cash return on investment each produces.

Starting with the property's gross scheduled income (GSI), we deduct for vacancies and uncollectible "losses," and are left with the gross operating income (GOI), which is the actual amount we have collected and have available to operate the property for the year. From the GOI, we then pay all the operating expenses, and we are left with the net operating income (NOI). If we paid cash for the property (and have no mortgages to be repaid), the NOI is our return on investment. If there are mortgages to repay, our return on investment is what remains after paying the debt service on those mortgages.

▶ **NOTE**

The NOI is what's left after paying the operating expenses, and it is the same number with-or-without mortgage expense.

Capitalization Rate or Cap Rate: The cap rate reflects the return on investment AFTER all operating expenses are paid, and it's expressed as a percentage return on investment, i.e.

Cap Rate = NOI ÷ Purchase Price/FMV =
Percentage Return on Investment

APOD: The property's annual property operating data should provide sufficient detail about the property such that we can see how it will perform for the first year of operation and determine its suitability as a candidate property to purchase. If not, ask the broker who prepared it any other questions you need answered before submitting an offer.

▶ **NOTE**

Be sure you are clear about what is actual data versus projected data provided because an APOD is NOT a certified representation of the property's current performance.

Debt Coverage Ratio or DCR: This is the lender's "safety factor" for minimizing the risk of a default in the payments due on a commercial loan. The lender requires the property to produce income in excess of the amount necessary to fully service the debt in order to reduce the lender's risk. DCR is usually pegged somewhere between 1.2 and 1.5 times the debt service. The higher the lender perceives the risk to be, the higher the DCR required to minimize his anxiety about the borrower's ability to repay the loan! Remember, with commercial loans (five units or more), the property's performance numbers are much more important to the lender than the borrower's personal numbers.

The Importance of Properly Valuing Properties

Whether you are a new investment property specialist or an investor, or both, your long-term success investing in real estate will absolutely depend upon your understanding and becoming good at valuing and evaluating properties, including making projections for the impact of changes you'll want or need to implement to improve that property's performance. In short, every property you find will not perform as well as the Mission Oaks Apartments, so be prepared to decide what you'll need to change to achieve better performance in the form of higher cash flow or higher market valuation for properties you want to add to your portfolio.

CHAPTER FIVE

Tax Benefits of Owning Real Estate

The Universal Investment Plan

No matter which vehicles you prefer when you invest your money, the simple, universal scenario we all hope for is to:

1. Make a large profit on the investment
2. Pay very little of that profit in taxes, and
3. Thereby retain as much of that profit as possible, to spend however we choose.

It certainly seems like a simple plan...perhaps a little too simple!

Because hope is not a strategy, and all investment opportunities are NOT created equal. Being selective about which investment vehicles you choose and focusing on those that provide high returns and advantageous tax treatment is a good place to begin.

The Case for Investing in Real Estate

One of the more attractive attributes of investing in real estate is that it is a tangible, real asset as opposed to some ethereal, mythical paper derivative that is not traceable to anything permanent. Real estate can usually be counted on to provide a continuing utility to its owner and user, regardless of variations in its monetary valuation. The fact that it also can provide high, tax-advantaged earnings and equity growth makes it a nearly ideal investment vehicle for many investors. Adding the benefit of utilizing leverage (or gearing, if you prefer) to magnify the gains we achieve provides an additional dimension to real estate investments not found elsewhere.

Tax Benefits of Owning Real Estate

Let's be clear. You will NOT automatically derive significant tax benefits from just any real estate you choose to own! You will only be highly compensated for investing in properties that are used in a trade or business or that provide occupancy for tenants who live in or work in your properties. This is the method your government uses to incentivize you to provide those facilities because everyone needs a place to live and to conduct their business (so they, too, can earn a living and pay their share of the cost of running our vast government). Fortunately, almost every type of real estate can be operated to produce cash flow and profits (i.e., operated as a business), so we have lots of candidate properties to choose from when that is our intent.

This does not mean that it's a bad idea to buy or inherit Grandma's farm simply because it probably doesn't provide the best tax incentives. You can derive immediate tax benefits from other properties in your portfolio and let the farm function as a family hideaway without ever turning it into a bed and breakfast or growing controversial crops.

Because the U.S. tax laws are both voluminous and complicated, it could be very costly to do your tax analysis and preparation yourself if you're not in the business. It makes far better sense to hire a competent professional to help you understand and maximize your tax benefits!

Investment real estate actually provides more tax benefits than almost any other type of investment, and to maximize your return on investment, it's important that you understand and pay attention to exactly what you can or cannot deduct as business expenses, starting with:

1. Interest Deductions

Mortgage interest deductions on loans used to purchase or repair your properties are often the largest expense of your business, but you also can deduct interest paid on credit cards, service charges, or personal loans attributable to your business activities.

2. Depreciation

Depreciation is sometimes called a phantom expense because it is not an actual, out of pocket cost, but rather, an allowance for the ultimate replacement of the buildings, fixtures, and improvements which comprise the property—all of which will wear out in time. The allowed depreciation is spread over a 27.5 year period for residential properties and over 39 years for commercial properties. But some of the fixtures, equipment, appliances, and landscaping are depreciable over much shorter periods, so consult your tax adviser for their recommendations about accelerating the depreciation on those components.

▶ **NOTE**

See the discussion about accelerated depreciation later in this chapter, for a more detailed explanation and sample calculations.

---

3. Repairs

Ordinary and reasonable repairs to keep your properties functioning properly are deductible expenses.

▶ **NOTE**

Don't do the repair work yourself! You cannot charge for your own labor, only for the materials and supplies you use. HIRE A REPAIRMAN!

---

4. Local or Long Distance Travel

Whether you drive or fly to your property to deal with tenants, speak to property managers, or to make repairs, you can deduct your actual expenses for airfare, hotels, meals, and other expenses. Document your expenses carefully to avoid unwarranted IRS attention and scrutiny.

5. Technical Training Seminars

Unfortunately, most of the training courses and seminars you attend to improve your knowledge about your real estate business are NOT allowed as tax deductible expenses.

(Reference IRS Publication 550 or discuss details of seminars and travel expenses with your CPA.)

Licensed real estate agents can deduct the costs of renewing their real estate license and their expenses for attending real estate trade association meetings as business expenses.

6. Home Office

You may deduct home office expenses or other devoted workspace used for your rental business, including computer software, internet, and phone service, whether you own or rent your home. You can also depreciate equipment used in your business, including computers, scanners, printers, cameras, etc.

▶ **NOTE**

Ask your CPA or tax attorney about the new first-year 100% deduction for up to $100,000 of business equipment purchased. If you are setting up or expanding your business, you can expense this equipment in the first year, rather than over the normal five year period. If you are an IPS, this is the perfect kind of tip to send to ALL your investor clients to make sure they discuss it with their tax advisor!

---

7. Employees/Independent Contractors

If you pay wages to an employee or an independent contractor, they are deductible as normal business expenses.

Employees: For employees, you will likely have to pay for any employer taxes due, withhold the employee's payroll deductions, and provide workers' compensation insurance.

Contractors: Most repairmen are independent contractors, so while no withholding is required, you will have to obtain the contractor's tax ID number and file IRS Form 1099 whenever you pay that contractor more than $600 in one tax year.

8. Theft and Casualty Losses

Depending on your specific insurance coverage, and the amount of damage you encounter from fire or flood losses, you may be able to deduct all or part of your loss.

9. Insurance

You can deduct the premiums paid for virtually all rental property insurance coverage, including fire, flood, theft, and landlord liability insurance. You can also deduct your employee's health insurance and workers' compensation insurance costs.

▶ **NOTE**

Make sure your insurance policy also includes loss of rents coverage which will make your mortgage payments while repairs are being made (in case you have an uninhabitable property with no tenant income with which to pay rents during a lengthy repair period). This extremely important coverage will only increase your insurance premiums by about 5%, and the possible benefits far outweigh the negligible cost factor.

10. Professional and Legal Services

You can deduct all fees paid for professional services rendered to your rental business by property managers, attorneys, accountants, and other professionals.

11. Becoming a Real Estate Professional

If you are a "real estate professional" who materially participates in managing your investment properties, you are permitted to take almost unlimited income tax deductions from those properties. This is a huge benefit, so we will examine exactly what it takes to become a "real estate professional" and whether you qualify to do so at the end of this chapter.

After Tax Cash Flow...How Sweet It Is!

It sounds like I'm excited about paying taxes on my earnings, and to a certain extent, that's true. However, while I do not want to pay any more than necessary, I REALLY don't want to pay "as little as possible," because to pay very little taxes, you simply have to make very little income. So even when I pay the minimum due, I'd still like that to be A LOT, because that is what will happen if I earn A LOT! So the idea here is not to earn less, but to earn more, and then to KEEP more of what we earn. Being a real estate investor helps us accomplish that goal because of the tax incentives we enjoy by providing rental properties that individuals or businesses can live or work in.

▶ **NOTE**

Before we look at my characterization of the specific benefits of owning investment real estate, it's important that you understand that I am neither a tax attorney nor a CPA, and I am therefore not qualified

to dispense advice on tax methods or practices you choose to employ with your real properties. My comments are drawn from my experience over some seven decades as a real estate investor and three and a half decades as a practicing real estate broker specializing in helping other investors buy, sell, manage, and exchange real properties in their portfolios. I urge you to consult your own personal tax consultant before relying upon any of my recommendations. A good rule of thumb is that you cannot consider information you receive from anyone as advice, unless you have paid them for it and they have specifically agreed to give you advice!

Tax Benefits of Real Estate Ownership

As we examine the investor's tax benefits in more detail, let me add a long-term perspective about the stability of those benefits. Over the several decades that I have been an active investor, I have seen MANY changes in the tax codes which directly affect the amount of taxes to be paid. In other words, you can expect tax amounts and rates to change regularly! But, don't despair; the tax codes giveth, the tax codes taketh away, and it will be ever thus. It will remain a moving platform, but the benefits outweigh the inconvenience, so you must learn to continue to pay attention to pending legislation that will impact the operation of your properties. Then you must be proactive about making adjustments that are needed to derive the most benefit. That will happen most easily when you have a permanent CPA or tax attorney working on your behalf and you habitually consult with them so that they can advise and alert you to impending changes. Their job is to tell you whether coming changes require action on your part or not.

Your Congress virtually always finds reason to change the rules of taxation, and I have personally seen significant swings in:

1. Individual tax bracket and income tax rates
2. Depreciation allowances and depreciation periods utilized for both commercial and residential properties
3. Huge variations in long-term capital gains tax rates, etc. Let your CPA and attorney worry about changes; you worry about taking advantage of the tax benefits that ARE available to you.

Generally, whatever the rates are when you put your properties into service tend to remain stable during the period you operate them. So most changes are NOT retroactive, allowing you to predict the tax benefits for individual properties in your portfolio.

So what are the specific tax benefits of real estate ownership? Let's start with what are probably the two most significant tax breaks available to U.S. taxpayers who own real estate.

1. The first tax benefit was not created for investors, but for homeowners, and it only applies to buying or selling your primary residence...*and it may be the best tax break in America!*

When our properties appreciate during our term of ownership, we normally pay capital gains tax when we sell, based upon the amount the value increases. But as homeowners, we are entitled to EXCLUDE up to $250,000 of the proceeds of the sale from those taxes.

You must have lived in the property—as your principal residence—for any two of the last five years prior to sale. This means you may rent out your home for up to three years prior to the sale and still qualify for the exclusion.

You can repeat this process again, as often as every two years, as many times as you choose to do so! So you can own and occupy several homes (sequentially) and exclude $250,000 of capital gains on each one you sell, spending the proceeds any way you like.

And YES, it's possible to own multiple rental properties simultaneously, which you convert from being rentals into your personal residence, one at a time, remodel, live there the required two-year minimum, sell it, exclude the capital gains, move into another one, and do it again...and again....

If you are married and are filing a joint return, you can exclude a total of $500,000 every two years, and two unmarried co-owners can independently exclude $250,000 each.

You are also allowed to deduct both your property taxes, and the interest paid on mortgages used to buy your principal residence, irrespective of whether or not you are selling your home.

2. The second best tax break in America was created for investors, and it involves obtaining special capital gains tax benefits upon sale of our rental properties, but happily, that's not all:

   a. We are also allowed to take deductions for expenses incurred in operating our rental businesses, including licensing fees, if applicable.

   b. We are allowed to deduct the interest paid on loans we use to acquire and to repair those rental properties.

   c. We are allowed to depreciate certain components of our rental properties, regardless of their actual physical condition.

   d. We are allowed and encouraged to use 1031 Tax-Deferred Exchanges to replace existing rental properties without having to pay capital gains taxes upon sale, which permits us to continue investing using all the property's appreciated equity.

      (A very detailed discussion of using 1031 Tax-Deferred Exchanges to build your investment portfolio is included in Chapter Six: How Do You Build and Manage a Real Estate Portfolio Successfully?)

   e. Investors can use their self-directed IRAs to purchase investment real estate or to fund mortgages or loans made to others that are secured by real estate.

So, let's examine exactly how our before tax cash flow (BTCF) is impacted by applying the appropriate tax benefits to determine our after tax cash flow (ATCF).

Accelerated Depreciation

It is first necessary for us to understand more about our ability to depreciate certain components of the property. The tax code allows us to deduct our losses for gradual deterioration of a material capital asset, no matter what its actual condition may be, and this is often referred to as a phantom loss because there is no out-of-pocket expense required to receive credit for this "loss." Moreover, with real property which has physical improvements (structures and landscape improvements), we are able to depreciate some of those components at accelerated rates, in proportion to their normal longevity.

For residential properties, the depreciation schedule for habitable buildings is currently 27.5 years; the land itself does not deteriorate, so it is not depreciable. Commercial properties are currently depreciated over a period of 39 years. Both residential and commercial properties normally contain equipment and additions which can be depreciated over much shorter time periods, due to their inherently shorter service lives.

As you will see, the ability to accelerate the depreciation of some of these property components can have a sizeable impact on our initial after tax cash flow (ATCF) when we purchase a new property.

Group I Components

The following items are depreciable over a five year service period:

1. Carpeting
2. Floor Coverings
3. Appliances
4. Window Air Conditioners
5. Draperies
6. Blinds
7. Furniture

Group II Components

These property improvements are depreciable over a fifteen year period:

1. Driveways
2. Carports
3. Landscaping
4. Patios
5. Fencing

So an important question you might ask about the depreciation allowance you are entitled to use for your property is, "Who determines the depreciation schedule I use?" And the answer is: YOU DO (with a bit of advice from your CPA). You are the only one who knows what components the property contains that are eligible for depreciation; and your CPA can help you decide what are reasonable allocations between fixtures, land, and land improvements for your specific property. Your job is to be consistent and it's probably prudent to be prepared to justify your approach or methodology in the event that you are ever audited.

The example below illustrates how we calculate these depreciation components as we determine their impact on our after tax cash flow (ATCF).

To do that, we will revisit the APOD we studied earlier in Chapter Four, which presented the salient features of a sizeable apartment complex called The Mission Oaks Apartments in Irvine, Texas. Based upon the data (see Figure 4) as supplied by the seller's agent, this particular property performs quite well BEFORE we consider its after tax performance. How can we evaluate the ATCF of this property?

Here's a brief review of its key parameters:

Purchase Price	GRM	Cap Rate
$4,500,000	6.73	10.26%

Cash Flow Analysis

Down Payment (26.67%): $1,200,000

First Loan: $3,150,000 (70% LTV) at 6.5% per annum, 30 years, 2 points

Second Loan: $150,000.00 (3.3% LTV) at 8.5% per annum, 25 years, 2 points

Before Tax Cash Flow (BTCF)

Monthly Income:	$59,489 per month	($713,865 per year)
– Expenses:	– $21,000 per month	($252,000 per year)
NOI:	$38,489 per month	($461,868 per year)
– Debt Service:	– $21,280 per month	($255,360 per year)

Net Spendable Income (NSI): $17,209 per month ($206,508 per year)[4]

Assumptions Used To Calculate Depreciation Allowances:

Component Allocations (as a percentage of total value of property)

[4] From the APOD, we've added one-time, first-year costs of first-year capital additions and replacement reserves totaling $80,000 to the initial investment required to simplify the calculations. This change stabilizes the BTCF at $17,209 per month for each year thereafter.

Component	Value	Percentage
Group I (Five year component) Allocation:	$350,000	7.8%
Group II (Fifteen year component) Allocation:	$200,000	4.4%
Value Allocation - All Buildings:	$3,330,000	74%
+ Value Allocation - Land (Not Depreciable):	+ $620,000	+ 13.8%
Total Property Value/Allocations:	$4,500,000	100%

▶ **NOTE**

The assumptions used to calculate depreciation allowances were chosen somewhat arbitrarily, and an argument could easily be made to employ different amounts or percentages for each depreciation group.

The total allowable depreciation is the sum of:

Group I: $350,000 ÷ 5 year = $ 70,000 per year for the first 5 years

Group II: $200,000 ÷ 15 year = $ 13,333 per year for the first 15 years

Buildings: $3,330,000 ÷ 27.5 year = $121,091 per year for 27.5 years

This means for the first through fifth years, the total depreciation allowance is the sum of all three groups, or:

Group I Depreciation Allowance:	$70,000 per year for first 5 years
Group II Depreciation Allowance:	$13,333 per year for first 5 years
+ Buildings Depreciation Allowance:	$121,091 per year for first 5 years
Total Depreciation Allowance:	$204,424 per year for first 5 years

For the next 10 years, the total depreciation allowance is the sum of the Group II and the building's depreciation, or $134,424 per year.

For the "final" 12.5 years, the depreciation allowance is that of the buildings alone, or $121,091 per year.

▶ **NOTE**

The total depreciation period for residential income property is 27.5 years. So after 27.5 years of ownership, you will have used up all your allowable depreciation. You are NEVER required to sell this property, BUT...if you still own it after 27.5 years, it's time to replace it and start a new depreciation period with the replacement property!

Let's assume our potential buyer is in a combined federal and state tax bracket of 35%. Using the allowable depreciation schedule above (for the first through fifth years), he can initially depreciate 35% of $204,424 per year, so his usable tax credit is

> $204,424 x 0.35 = $71,548 per year (or $5,962 per month).

After Tax Cash Flow (ATCF)

This means the buyer's ATCF is now the sum of his net spendable income (NSI) plus his usable tax credit, or

> ATCF = $206,508 (NSI) + $71,548 (tax credit) = $278,056 per year or $23,171 per month,

for the first five years, presuming rents and expenses are stable! This is a whopping 21+% overall cash-on-cash return on his initial investment! At the end of the first five year period, this investor will have received ALL OF HIS INITIAL INVESTMENT BACK, PLUS he will have paid for $50,000 in planned improvements and $30,000 for replacement of reserves.

...And for the next 10 years, he continues to receive ATCF of

> $206,508 per year (NSI) + a tax credit of $134, 424 per year x 0.35, which is $47,066 per year,

so his total annual ATCF is now

> $206,508 (NSI) + $47,066 per year (tax credit) = $253,574 per year, or $21,131 per month

How long would YOU want to receive this monthly cash flow with nothing invested?

▶ NOTE

Perhaps a better way to look at this scenario is that the investor received his *entire initial investment* back in five years, so he now has NO CASH INVESTED, and he is therefore receiving all future cash flow at an INFINITE rate of return on his investment! That's a good number!

And finally, after a total of 15 years in the property, his ATCF cash flow drops again for the remaining 12.5 years, to

$206,508 (NSI) + a tax credit of ($121,091 per year x .035) =
$206,508 per year + $42,382 per year =
$248,890 per year, or $20,741 per month

So, sometime before the final 12.5 years expires, this investor will need to find a replacement property to exchange for this property so he can continue this real, live game of Monopoly, and start all over again depreciating his new replacement property for at least another 27.5 years.

Suppose We DIDN'T Use Accelerated Depreciation

What would the result have been if we DID NOT use the accelerated depreciation available to the Group I and Group II components? Suppose we merely depreciated the buildings using a value of 80% for the buildings and 20% for the land? In that scenario, the depreciation benefit would remain fixed (up to 27.5 years) at an amount of:

Depreciation Allowance = $4,500,000 x 0.8 ÷ 27.5, which is $130,909 per year, or $10,909 per month

In his 35% tax bracket, the investor's tax credit will be:
$130.909 x 0.35 = $45,818 per year, or $3,818 per month

His ATCF now becomes:
$17,209 per month (NSI) + $3,818 per month = $21,027 per month

Surprisingly, this is still a 19% or more cash on cash return, and the initial difference (without accelerated depreciation) is only $2,144 per month less. Still...$2,144 per month for 60 months is an additional $128,660 in the first five years. That should certainly help pay for a good CPA to help create the higher yield!

For an accurate comparison of utilizing the accelerated depreciation allowance, versus the straight-line depreciation, presuming the buyer retained the property for the full depreciation period, here's what we have:

Accelerated Depreciation:

Years 1 thru 5:	$23,171 per month x 60 months	=	$1,390,260
Years 6 thru 15:	$21,131 per month x 120 months	=	$2,535,720
+ Years 16 thru 27.5:	$20,741 per month x 150 months	=	$3,111,150
	Total Accelerated Depreciation Allowance:		$7,037,130

Straight-Line Depreciation:

Years 1 thru 27.5: $21,027 per month x 27.5 years x 12 months = $6,938,910

The actual difference over the full 27.5 year period is only $98,220

It's not a LOT of money, but, you'd likely find a use for it!

Is After Tax Cash Flow the Whole Story?

No, it's definitely not the whole story. We've only looked at the CASH FLOW portion of the income that occurs from owning and operating this property over a 20+ year time period. What about the owner's equity over that same period? We haven't even considered what will have happened as a result of increases in the rental income over the same 20 year period.

Suppose that the net income were to increase a modest 2% per year? After 20 years, the rental income will have risen by about 50%, meaning that:

1. The investor's actual cash-on-cash return would then be up to $25,814 per month, which is 22% or more return per year on initial investment, and...

2. The property's total value will have increased to something over $6,750,000 (based on its higher income), representing new equity of approximately $2,250,000, in addition to the operating cash flow.

Equity gain also arises from loan amortization paydown, which occurs when the tenants are paying down the principal portion of the loans. After 20 years, the combined loan balances will now be paid down to about $1,812,308, so the investor has also gained:

$3,300,000 - $1,812,308 = $1,487,692

in new equity due to principal pay down.

Yes, in addition to the ongoing cash flow from operating the property, the investor's equity is now comprised of:

a. his initial down payment of $1,200,000, plus the initial $80,000 spent on first-year capital additions and replacement reserves
b. equity increase due to market appreciation of about $2,250,000, plus
c. equity gained due to amortization (loan pay down) of $1,487,000.

So now his total equity after 20+ years of ownership is approximately the sum of a. + b. + c., which is:

$1,200,000	Down Payment
$80,000	Reserves
$2,250,000	Market Appreciation
+ $1,487,000	Loan Principal Paydown

Total Buyer's Equity: $5,017,000 (which is $517,000 more than he paid for the apartment buildings initially!)

Of course, there are many other variables and we can continue to conjecture about future value based upon what is likely to happen, but only time will reveal the actual results. Suffice it to say, this is a property that will undoubtedly continue to perform quite well, and we would do well to have it and several others like it in our own portfolios!

▶ **NOTE**

This may have seemed like a whirlwind analysis, especially if you haven't done similar calculations before. The numbers are large, but the methods are straightforward, so take your time reviewing them so that you understand the process.

Is This a Realistic Scenario for This Property?

Actually, the numbers revealed in our review of the ATCF benefits of The Mission Oaks Apartments are dramatic, so note that not every property you analyze is going to perform so well over an extended period. The extraordinary cash-on-cash return rates are possible here because of the multiplication factor provided by leveraging the buyer's down payment by almost 4:1 (purchase price divided by down payment of 26.67%), which is not available in non-real estate investments.

This property does perform very well because it is offered for sale at a price and with in-place financing that allows the buyer the ability to purchase and operate it with:

1. a low GRM of 6.73
2. a high cap rate of 10.26%
3. loans in-place providing 70% LTV with attractive rates that allow a cash-on-cash return of 11.56%.

A combination of being able to buy a good property with good terms, plus benefiting from the financing leverage common to investment real estate purchases, plus taking advantage of the tax benefits of depreciation produces a scenario we'd enjoy repeating often.

It is a common plan for investors who specialize in larger apartment complexes to be able to buy such a property, spend serious time, money, and effort to force equity, then refinance it to pull that equity back out. They then end up in exactly the same position of having little or no funds still invested, therefore obtaining near infinite cash flow return. The difference here is that the Mission Oaks Apartments simply did not require the hard work and upgrades that are usually necessary to achieve those results.

Should You Hold The Mission Oaks Apartments as a Cash Cow for 27.5 Years?

Although it would be very tempting to simply take the cash each month, I think doing so could be considered mismanagement of this asset unless you also put those funds to work for you. Essentially, the cash flow becomes free money after five years which can be used to debt service loans (on other leveraged properties) or fund other projects while your equity in this property continues to grow. There will certainly be many targets of opportunity available to you which could benefit from a long-term steady cash flow which this property can provide!

Should YOU Become a "Real Estate Professional?"

This book was written primarily for two groups of people:

1. Real Estate Agents

The first group is real estate agents who want to become investment property specialists (IPSs), who will be able to enjoy an extraordinary career assisting real estate investors while learning to invest for themselves and becoming wealthy from those investments. As an IPS YOU can "get rich in this niche" because it's very existence is a virtual secret in the agent community, and there is almost no competition from anyone for these investor's business! This group can easily demonstrate that they already are or can quickly become "real estate professionals."

2. Real Estate Investors

The second group is real estate investors who will become increasingly successful in understanding how to build and operate a portfolio of properties that will help them obtain—and sustain—the exceptional lifestyle that's available to those investors who can envision and create what they want. Many of these investors can also qualify as "real estate professionals."

Whether you are a brand new agent, a seasoned veteran, or a full-time real estate investor, many of you are in a unique position to take advantage of the EXTRA tax benefits that are only available to "real estate professionals!" The path to becoming a "real estate professional" as an IPS, however, has a separate set of rules that agents must adhere to, which we will need to understand thoroughly before we begin that path.

So what does it take to become a "real estate professional," and why is it worth pursuing, whichever path you take?

A "real estate professional" is a tax classification used by the IRS to describe a person who spends at least 750 hours a year "materially participating" in the management of his investment properties, and that participation in real estate must also be his principal activity (more than 50% of his work effort must be spent on real estate activities). Materially participating includes supervision (of employees, contractors, and property managers) or meeting (with brokers, accountants, private or public planners, financial advisors, architects, tradespeople, and municipalities) in pursuit of projects or properties you build, construct, redesign, update, own, and operate, etc. It is not necessary to be a licensed real estate agent! No, you are not required to sell someone else's properties or hold open houses for the rest of your career!

Realistically, however, it may be easier to earn the "real estate professional" classification as a building contractor or as a real estate licensee who sells, leases, and manages properties simply because it's easier to show that real estate is definitely your principal activity. But investors who can demonstrate that they or their spouses spend more than 50% of their time on real estate and that their combined hours of participation are adequate can qualify together...and it's well worth the effort!

Thanks to the magic of depreciation credits, real estate investors are commonly able to operate their properties and receive positive net cash flow while still showing a net loss after taxes, and those who qualify as "real estate professionals" will be able to utilize nearly unlimited amounts of loss to offset their income from other sources regardless of the absolute amounts of either the income or the loss.

If you are NOT a "real estate professional," you will be restricted to using the "passive loss limitations," which allow write-offs of up to $25,000 per year against your other income provided your adjusted gross income is not more than $100,000 per year. Unfortunately, that benefit reduces linearly to zero, when your income reaches $150,000 per year, and thereafter, you have no allowable write-offs at all.

To make it worse, Congress added a new windfall tax called the net investment income tax (NII Tax) in 2013 which is a separate, flat 3.8% income tax on unearned income, including rental income and gains from selling rental property. This tax applies specifically to higher net worth real estate investors whose adjusted gross income is greater than $200,000 per year for singles or greater than $250,000 per year if married or filing jointly ($125,000 for married couples filing separately). The good news is that the NII tax doesn't apply to "real estate professionals."

I'm sure you are beginning to see why I think it's worthwhile to consider becoming a real estate professional if you can qualify. In my own personal case, although I've been a real estate broker for over 38 years, my wife could have qualified as a real estate professional on her own because of the time she spent managing our personal properties even though she was not a licensed agent. She maintained a full-time dedicated office at one of our properties from which she supervised employees, hired repairmen and contractors, and managed several other rental properties.

If you are a real estate investor with a full-time job who is not in a real estate business, you cannot qualify as a real estate professional. If, however, you are married and file a joint return, your spouse can still qualify BOTH of you based on the time she works in the real estate business. She can spend time managing your properties, (and even become a part-time real estate agent if necessary) to meet the 750 hour and the 50% or more time requirements. Your hours can be combined with hers to meet the material participation requirement of actively managing your properties. This step will ensure that neither the passive loss rules nor NII tax will apply to you.

If you are a real estate investor with a full-time job in a real estate business, you can easily qualify as a real estate professional; if you are an agent, you must work inside the framework that applies to all agents who work in countries and states where agents must be licensed. In other words, you must either be a licensed real estate broker yourself or you must work under the supervision of a licensed broker. Most licensing jurisdictions will require you to serve a two-year apprenticeship as an agent before you can become a broker yourself and work without further supervision.

Why is that a problem? It's not necessarily a problem, but it will require a frank discussion with your new broker to make sure your plans are mutually compatible. Most brokers will welcome your participation in the business as an investor, but his business probably wasn't established to supervise investor agents, so he'll be more enthusiastic about supervising you if you are a salesperson whose plan entails earning commissions by selling properties to and for the investor clients you represent. That is how your broker gets paid, by splitting the sales commissions you earn, which allows him to help support his office with staff, computers, technical tools, training, and advertising. His success depends upon your success, and that can easily be measured by the number of transactions you complete.

As a beginning, rookie agent, you will commonly be offered a real estate commission "split" of about 50% to you, 50% to the broker. Be sure to ask for and expect to get technical training and assistance at that stage. As you advance in skills and sales, your split will gradually increase, and depending upon your sales volume and experience, you can expect to earn somewhere between 65% to 70% with seriously contributing pros eventually reaching up to 90% splits.

While your broker does not have any involvement in your personal property ownership or investment property activities, he is still liable for your professional conduct, so don't expect him to allow you to conduct a property management business in his offices. He does not want that liability.

You may find that—depending upon your focus and business activities—you can comfortably operate your business while working for your broker indefinitely. You can continue to share revenues and operate from his office without assuming the responsibility of owner or manager as long as you choose (and as long as you are both content with the arrangement). Or, you can ultimately decide to get your own broker's license, own your own business and office building, and neither share revenues nor require his supervision as you grow your business.

I have followed both of these paths, with the only variation being that I was already a broker when I joined my first company as a rookie agent who definitely needed training, supervision, and assistance, as I described in Chapter Two: Lessons Learned From My First Investment Property Transaction as a Real Estate Agent. The point I want to emphasize here is that although I had accumulated over 20 years experience as a real estate investor, I had NONE as an agent, and I definitely had a lot to learn about becoming an IPS!

Throughout my career as an investment property specialist, I was able to successfully focus on serving other investors while working as the broker-of-record for myself or as a broker associate in another broker's office where they specialized in residential real estate sales.

Why do I insist that becoming a "real estate professional" is worthwhile for you? Because it's not that hard to do compared to the benefits you'll receive. Either path to becoming a "real estate professional" will work if you qualify, and the major reason to pursue the designation is that it will materially affect your growth rate as an investor, simply because you get to keep more of the money you earn, and you get to keep those funds working for you as you build your real estate empire—it will simply happen much faster!

CHAPTER SIX

How Do You Build and Manage a Real Estate Portfolio Successfully?

In Chapter Three: Understanding Investment Properties, we discussed creating a written plan to help us clarify WHY we selected real estate as our vehicle of choice to build a retirement portfolio, and we asked the key question, "What do you want your real estate investments to do for you?"

If you answered, "Make me wealthy!" that's interesting, but far too vague! It doesn't address the specific results necessary to make it measurable (and therefore attainable), like:

How?

Have you developed a specific goal you want to attain (measured in units, fair market value, equity, annual cash flow, or otherwise)?

Have you determined your target for monthly cash flow that will be necessary to sustain the lifestyle you are creating for yourself? How much will you need? By when?

When?

What is a realistic timetable to acquire the necessary portfolio of properties you'll need to produce the income or net worth you want? Have you established the specific property types and unit mix you want to own?

Where?

Have you determined where you will invest? Or will you instead simply plan to acquire the "targets of opportunity" that you find in the marketplace?

What?

Which asset classes, vehicles, or property types do you plan to use?

What is your long-term investment plan?

What will the outcome look like when you have reached your goal? And what is your exit strategy when you are finished?

You may not be able to answer all of these questions if you are just now formulating your plan, but it's important that you consider the questions and begin to determine, as best you can, how you plan to start or to increase your portfolio.

The more specific you can be, the more this looks like a GOAL instead of a WISH. The more measurable your plan's objectives are, the clearer they become, and the better you can focus on attaining them.

Even if you have very clearly determined your personal investment philosophy before you start on your investment path, you should be prepared for a tendency to shift your plan somewhat as you continue to implement it. Don't be alarmed. It's what we all do as we learn more about the realities of our task and sometimes realize that a few changes will improve things. In fact, gradual changes may become your new normality.

What Types of Real Estate COULD You Choose to Invest In?

Now, let's add some confusion to the mix. You may now be thinking that the most direct path to rental property ownership is to systematically begin to acquire some single-family residences and gradually trade those for, or keep them and add additional, smaller multifamily units, eventually moving to larger multifamily units, thus creating both ongoing cash flow and building equity in them over time.

That's not a bad plan! If you follow the rules of sound financing and good stewardship and provide places for your happy tenants to live, you should be able to achieve a strong portfolio of investment properties that will serve you well over time. In fact, this is how most real estate investors begin, usually buying properties close to home. So it's a tried and true formula. But it's not the only formula, so let's consider for a moment some of the other ways we can invest in real estate and what the trade-offs might be in selecting other property types or related business opportunities as our vehicles of choice.

Here are some examples of both common and peripheral investment vehicles used by real estate investors. You will note that many of them combine running businesses in conjunction with owning the property that houses the business:

Residential

1. Condos or single-family homes (refurbish to add value)[5]
2. Vacation resort rentals (from beach locations to alpine ski lodges)
3. Timeshare resorts or fractional ownership vacation properties (build new or buy and operate only)
4. Daycare centers for children or seniors, assisted living facilities, or full-care nursing homes
5. Rehabilitation homes or centers for drug dependency or needy families
6. Bed and breakfast inns or small hotels
7. Specialty fishing, diving, hunting camps, excursions
8. Mobile home parks or overnight motorhome, camper parks
9. Single-family homes or large multi-unit apartment buildings

If you have the capacity and inclination, you may choose to be the hands-on operator of these businesses, or instead, you may simply own the property and hire an operator or lease the property to an operator who runs the business. If you already operate a business or choose to start a new business, it is almost always a good plan to own the buildings that house your businesses. The tax benefits of ownership help pay for them, and you are permanently in control of where your business is located.

[5] The question with these properties is, are you keeping them for the production of income? If you add value to them, but resell them without renting them, you are considered to be a dealer, not an investor, and any profit you make will be taxed as ordinary income. So you cannot be a flipper or wholesaler and get capital gains treatment until you are in a position to keep some of these properties "long-term." If you indeed hold them and rent them to tenants, you can now take the tax benefits of depreciation, etc.

Non-Residential

(These tenants generally take less care and feeding than residential tenants.)

1. Public storage facilities (develop or own property and run or lease business)
2. Retail shopping space, restaurants, office space, warehouses
3. Urban parking lots or garages
4. Leasable farmlands, billboards, cell towers atop your buildings

Private Syndications

If you have sufficient experience and ability, you can create private syndications which allow other investors to participate with you in the investment vehicles you design. This is often a great way to increase the size and complexity of your next project and to begin to acquire happy investors who want to do it again!

Syndications can readily accelerate the rate at which you can grow your business by combining the skills you have or will learn with the resources of other participants to help expand both the scale and pace of your business activity and acumen while providing your investors opportunities they would not be able to realize by themselves.

We will examine syndication opportunities in more detail in Chapter Seven: Should Your Investment Strategy Include Taking on Partners?

▶ NOTE

CAUTION: Be aware that whenever you accept and manage investor funds with an expectation of a return on that investment, you are dealing with a security, and you must comply with all federal and state security laws. Be sure to engage the services of an attorney who is familiar with securities regulations to ensure that your syndication complies with all appropriate regulations.

Other Opportunities Peripheral to Direct Real Estate Investments

1. **Real Estate Investment Trusts (REITS):** REITS are a more likely vehicle to use for your exit strategy than for the acquisition phase of your real estate portfolio, but they are legitimate real estate investments which deliver returns to owners. REITS have been around for more than 60 years, and ownership is achieved by buying stock in a REIT corporation, which earns money by either investing in ownership of large real estate projects or by providing mortgages for these projects. There are both public and privately traded REITS available is several countries with a collective market value of greater than a trillion dollars. U.S. tax law permits IRS 1031 tax-deferred exchanges of real estate assets into and out of REITS, which is why they are used in the exit strategies of retiring investors who decide they want to continue to invest in real estate but prefer to assume a totally passive role in the future.

2. **Hard Money Lending:** Hard money loans are made to real estate investors who usually need funds sooner rather than later. These investors are willing or required to pay a higher price for hard money loans than they would for funds borrowed from conventional banks or commercial lenders. It is commonplace for hard money lenders to charge significantly higher interest rates as well as higher points and fees for their loans, which are secured by the subject property or other collateral. The loans may be the senior or only loan on the property, but are more often junior loans, with commensurately higher rates, as a function of risk anticipated or the total loan-to-value of the combined loans. Hard money loans are usually completed quickly, so they may well be worth the higher cost to investors in exchange for quicker funding and a simpler process.

   You can place your funds through a loan broker who specializes in hard money transactions. Or you can choose to become a licensed broker yourself, which allows you to place funds for yourself and for other investors. A great way to obtain high returns on your self-directed IRA funds is to provide loans to other real estate investors.

See Chapter Eight: Using SDIRAs to Buy Investment Real Estate for more information on investing or lending your IRA funds.

3. **Tax Lien Certificates and Tax Deed Sales:** Tax Lien Certificates and Tax Deed Sales are NOT direct investments in real estate per se. Rather, they are based upon a city or other municipality's need to continue to operate even when property taxes go unpaid by property owners. Here, the investor essentially pays the delinquent property taxes in lieu of the delinquent property owner and when the taxpayer finally pays his delinquent tax bill, the investor keeps the interest paid, WHICH IS USUALLY AT DOUBLE DIGIT RATES. The risk involved is minimal. The investor gets good returns and may even end up keeping the property in the event of nonpayment by the taxpayer. Tax lien certificates and tax deed sales are available on both residential and commercial properties in thousands of municipalities across the U.S.

If you're not familiar with tax lien certificates and tax deed sales look at the explanation in the Glossary of Terms, or refer to *The 16% Solution* by Joel Moskowitz recommended reading section at the end of this chapter.

And these are only the tip of the iceberg! There are innumerable ways to invest in real estate, or real estate related projects. There is not a wrong way or a right way. Virtually any property can work as an investment vehicle if it has the ability to provide cash flow. You need only choose a product that you've spent sufficient time and energy researching and for which you understand the marketplace thoroughly before you begin. It's even possible that your geographical area may offer unique options. Be certain to consider the sustainability of the income stream you select to purchase.

Whichever path you take and whatever mix of properties you acquire, you will have similar decisions to make about settling on an exit strategy when you are finished building your real estate empire. Figuring out what your exit strategy is going to be is an important, but often overlooked, part of designing your long-term plan. A lot of hard work will be required to establish a successful property portfolio, and determining your exit strategy in advance will serve to prove that the effort required was indeed worthwhile!

We will discuss specific exit strategies later in this chapter. Before you get to that stage, however, you are likely to have many opportunities and perhaps many decisions to make about the changes you'll want to implement in reshaping your growing portfolio over the years. Because I'm a buy-and-hold investor, I personally think it's a great idea to acquire new properties without having to sell the ones you already own, if you have that option. Generally, I want to increase my assets by adding additional properties to my holdings. But, there are definitely times when just replacing an existing property is appropriate, so let's look at why, and under what circumstances, we would do that.

▶ **NOTE**

Please be aware that I am neither a CPA or tax advisor, nor am I an attorney, and I am definitely NOT qualified to give you individual tax advice. What I am presenting here are observations and experiences based upon my 38+ years as a practicing real estate broker assisting real estate investors in my role as an IPS. Before you decide to utilize any of these strategies, consult your personal tax attorney or CPA for their specific advice.

Learning to Use 1031 Tax-Deferred Exchanges

In the United States, our favorite method for changing or replacing the properties in our portfolio is to utilize an IRS 1031 tax-deferred exchange. This is a provision in the U.S. tax code which allows an investor to defer capital gains tax due upon the sale of an appreciated investment property by using the equity in the property to purchase another income property (or group of properties) to replace it. There are a significant number of rules to be followed when executing a proper exchange, so it's imperative that you work closely with your tax advisor, and with an experienced exchange intermediary when planning and executing a 1031 tax-deferred exchange.

Why should investors learn to understand this particular portion of the tax code? Because it was devised exclusively for their benefit!

So How Is a 1031 Tax-Deferred Exchange Accomplished?

When an investor decides to sell an investment property and engage in a 1031 exchange, he starts by contacting a qualified intermediary (QI) and they enter into an exchange agreement.

The investment property is then put on the market and offered for sale.

When an offer to purchase the property is accepted and signed by the qualified intermediary (QI), escrow for the sale is opened, and a preliminary title report is produced.

Then the qualified intermediary (QI) prepares and sends the required exchange documentation to the escrow closer for signing at the property closing.

Escrow closes (on the property the exchanger relinquishes), and the exchange period clock starts ticking. The exchanger now has 180 days to identify and close escrow on the replacement property he selects.

During the first 45 days after the close of escrow on the relinquished property, the investor (who we are identifying as the exchanger) identifies replacement properties as required by law. This is known as the identification period.

Within 180 days after the close of escrow on the relinquished property, the investor closes on one or more of the replacement properties he has identified. This is called the exchange period. This completes the exchange. In a perfect exchange, no cash from the transaction—or boot, as it is known—is normally taken by the exchanger. If cash or other boot IS accepted by the exchanger, a portion of the capital gains will be due immediately instead of being deferred until a later time period.

The Basics of Using 1031 Tax-Deferred Exchanges

One of the two best tax breaks available to U.S. investors is the ability to utilize 1031 tax-deferred exchanges to help build our real estate portfolios. This section of the tax code gives us the opportunity to reposition our assets by exchanging one property for another property without having to immediately pay the taxes that have accrued due to the capital gains growth of the first property. This is a huge benefit which we should learn to utilize whenever the opportunity exists, and here's why it's so important:

Assume I own a property (that I've held for more than one year), and it has increased in value over that time from $100,000 (original acquisition cost) to a current value of $300,000. If I sell it outright, I will pay for:

1. Sales costs of approximately $24,000 (8%) +

2. Capital gains tax on the net gain at a 15% tax rate:

Selling Price:	$300,000
Less Acquisition Cost:	– $100,000
Less Sales Expense:	– $ 24,000
Net Capital Gains:	$176,000

Capital gains tax due upon sale:
$176,000.00 x 15% = $26,400

So, after the sale, I am left with:

Proceeds of Sale:	$300,000
Less Sales Expenses:	– $ 24,000
Less Capital Gains Tax Paid:	– $ 26,400
Available Net Proceeds to Spend on New Property	$249,600

Since my intention all along was to buy a replacement property from the proceeds of the sale, suppose that instead of doing an outright sale, I elect to do a 1031 tax-deferred exchange of the property? What are the advantages?

The primary advantage is that I can now defer paying the capital gains tax of $26,400 until sometime in the future, which allows me to use those proceeds NOW as additional down payment on the replacement properties I'm buying! So utilizing the 1031 tax-deferred exchange and deferring the $26,400 fee allows me to transfer $276,000 (instead of $249,600) to the purchase of the new replacement properties!

This means that I can either buy a more expensive replacement property or perhaps obtain a smaller loan on the new property. Moreover, I am entitled to exchange a single property for a group of properties, or exchange multiple properties for a single larger or smaller property, or exchange a group of properties for another group, etc. Practically, that means I can divert the $26,400 into a separate property, as long as it's a part of the exchange.

You get the idea; I can be quite creative, although I don't want to structure an exchange that is so complicated I run the danger of not completing it because one of the pieces couldn't be closed along with the rest of them! That would be a mistake, because no matter what I intended, if I don't adhere to the precise exchange rules, my transaction will be ruled to be a sale and a purchase—NOT an exchange—and the $26,400 tax will be due in the year of sale.

By the way, I do not have the option of merely pocketing the $26,400 because that is considered "boot" in the exchange, which is also a taxable event. Although the details of what is and isn't permissible in a proper exchange are slightly tedious, we will review them in detail in the next section.

▶ NOTE

The above calculations utilized a capital gains tax rate of 15% to illustrate the importance of deferring the tax thereby enabling the use of those funds NOW to acquire your replacement property. For 2016, the minimum capital gains tax rate is 0%. The actual rate applied depends upon the seller's individual tax bracket, which is in turn dependent upon the seller's taxable income. Today, for sellers in the 10-15% tax bracket, the capital gains tax rate is 0%. For sellers in the 25-35% tax bracket, the capital gains tax rate is 15%, and for sellers in the 39.6% tax bracket, the capital gains tax rate is 20% for residential properties and 25% for commercial properties. Don't bother to memorize these numbers. They will change often at the whim of your Congress. Be sure to check with your tax advisor to determine your applicable tax ramifications of a sale or exchange!

Using 1031 Tax-Deferred Exchanges to Help Build Your Portfolio

There are several reasons why we might sell a perfectly good asset. The most common one is because we have held it long enough to have used all the allowable depreciation on this property. So if we merely complete a 1031 exchange to replace it with another property of equal or higher value, we get to start all over again depreciating the new property without penalties, and again we can defer paying the taxes that have accrued due to capital gains on the relinquished property.

Sometimes we can upgrade a property by utilizing a 1031 exchange to acquire a newer building with less upkeep or maintenance required, especially if it becomes difficult to refinance the older property to optimize our debt-to-earnings ratio or to free up capital for other investments. I firmly believe that optimizing the financing allows us to get a far better return on money invested by operating more efficiently. In other words, buckets of cash flow may sound good, but this happens at the expense of your having excessive equity in the property, which occurs because the property is inadequately leveraged. You might call this mismanaging your portfolio.

Mismanaging Your Portfolio Can Be VERY Expensive

I'd like to share an example from my personal experience that illustrates just how expensive it can be to mismanage your portfolio.

My brother and I owned and operated a 50-unit apartment building near San Jose State University which we kept for 25 years. It was a class C property in poor condition when we bought it, but over the years, we improved it, and of course, the rents and the building's value increased considerably.

Bill and I were both working engineers who owned other investment properties, so as cash flow to the apartment building increased, we largely ignored it, because we didn't really need the building's cash flow in our individual budgets, and we weren't paying close enough attention to realize that we should have traded it at least once, or maybe twice, during our ownership.

We bought the building for approximately $235,000 in 1977, and we sold it for $2,600,000 in 2003. The mortgage balance was only about $400,000, so it was hemorrhaging cash flow! Nice! Those are good numbers! Sounds like a great success story. But that's the simple view. Let's look a little closer....

Had we been smart enough to refinance it *and*

1. Acquire additional properties with those funds, *and*
2. Had we also done at least one 1031 exchange during those 25 years, we would probably have realized at least a $20,000,000 return. (My son Robert estimates that potential return at well over $40,000,000.)

You see why I believe too much cash flow is NOT such a good thing!

The lesson here is that because we didn't need the money—and therefore we were not paying enough attention to the opportunity—we simply were not prepared to take what the market was ready to give us. Obviously we needed to take action to derive the benefit that was available. I hope you will learn from our mistake and not let this happen to you! To be sure, we want our properties to deliver sustainable, positive cash flow...but maybe not buckets full!

So, back to using 1031 exchanges, the main idea here is that we do not want to have to sell an existing asset because it will invariably have accrued some capital gains, and a sale will trigger a taxable event where Uncle Sam wants to share in the profits from the sale. (No, he won't share in your losses if the building has somehow shriveled in value.)

Instead of a sale, we want to create a 1031 tax-deferred exchange, wherein we relinquish the property we are giving up and replace it with a more suitable property that we are going to operate instead. The properties we exchange via a 1031 exchange are commonly called the downleg (relinquished) property and the upleg (replacement) property.

By utilizing this exchange, we avoid paying tax on the relinquished property in the year of the sale and are able to transfer ALL those tax-deferred funds directly into our equity in the new replacement property. So why is that such a big deal, if we must ultimately pay the tax anyhow?

We now get to continue operating the new property at a much improved financial advantage because we paid no tax to Uncle Sam (it was deferred). We have those funds at our disposal in the form of equity transferred to the new property, so our new loan, if any, will costs us less, and the new property will perform far better financially, with or without debt.

The idea here is NOT to shortchange Uncle Sam. It is to pay him everything he is owed...BUT NOT NOW! We get FREE use of that tax-deferred money NOW, and we pay Uncle Sam later. This will make a significant difference in the amount of property you are able to acquire in your real estate portfolio over time because every exchange you do allows you to purchase the upleg properties using money you would have paid in taxes without the benefit of the exchange!

Why do you suppose such a benefit has been created by the U.S. government for real property investors? The answer is simply that offering this incentive is what ensures that investors will indeed continue to invest in properties that provide rental housing or office space for people and jobs for those who manage and operate those properties.

What Type of Real Property Qualifies for a 1031 Tax-Deferred Exchange?

Only properties that are *held for business use or for investment purposes (for the production of income)* are suitable for 1031 exchanges, and they must be like-kind properties. What are like-kind properties? Essentially, ANY real property held for investment or real property used in a trade or business can be exchanged for ANY other real property held for investment or real property used in a trade or business. Happily, virtually ALL real estate is essentially like-kind, so any real property you plan to hold for the production of income qualifies.

Exchanges of items other than real estate are also possible, but those exchanges are not a topic for this discussion. Consult your tax advisor for details.

▶ **NOTE**

IPSs need to pay particular attention to learning the rules of 1031 tax-deferred exchanges because they will be required to assist their investors many times in their quest to become more valuable IPSs. There is lots of information and plenty of assistance available from professional exchange intermediaries on specific transactions, but a basic understanding of the rules will make your life simpler as both an agent and as an investor.

The Rules We Need to Understand About 1031 Tax-Deferred Exchanges

The rules of 1031 exchanges are not particularly difficult, but they are definite and specific and require precise interpretation to be judged as a proper and allowable exchange. As you will see, while it's important what your intent is with respect to an exchange, you MUST obey the rules precisely to effect your exchange of properties.

Let's start by defining some of the terms used in the exchange. Four individuals or entities will be considered parties to the exchange.

If you are the person or entity who sells (relinquishes) Property A and who then purchases (replaces it with) Property B, you are called the exchanger. In addition to the sales contract and the purchase contract, there is also an exchange contract connecting these two properties. The first thing we must be sure to do correctly is consistently identify the exchanger in the sales and purchase contracts to be certain they are one and the same. That is, the person or entity that relinquishes the title to Property A must be the SAME person or entity that takes the title to Property B.

The other three parties to the exchange are the buyer of Property A, the seller of Property B, and the accommodator or qualified intermediary.

Whenever we perform a 1031 exchange, we ALWAYS want to use the services of a qualified intermediary (QI) (also know as an accommodator) to assist us in handling the transaction correctly. The QI must be registered with the IRS and cannot be related to the exchanger or have been associated with him in business for at least a two year period. This essentially precludes the use of the exchanger's personal attorney, CPA, or real estate agent as the QI. The QI is required to execute an exchange agreement with the exchanger and to act as a fiduciary who ensures that the exchanger does not receive constructive receipt of the transferred funds before escrow is closed and title to Property B is transferred to the exchanger.

In order for the exchange to be completely tax-deferred, the replacement property must:

1. Be of equal or higher value than the relinquished property
2. Be acquired with equal or more equity than the relinquished property
3. Be acquired with equal or more debt than the relinquished property, or the shortfall must be replaced with cash from outside the exchange.

If any of these conditions are not met, the exchange can be completed, but the exchanger is considered to have received boot equal to the total amount of the imbalances, so tax will be due on the aggregate difference.

Here are some common examples of boot calculations in an exchange:

Example 1: Exchanger goes up in value, across in equity, and up in mortgage:

	RELINQUISHED	**REPLACEMENT**
Value	$ 150,000	$225,000
Equity	$ 50,000	$ 50,000
Mortgage	$ 100,000	$175,000

RESULT: No tax is due here because all conditions for deferral are met.

Example 2: Exchanger goes up in value, down in equity, keeps $10,000 of proceeds:

	RELINQUISHED	**REPLACEMENT**
Value	$ 150,000	$225,000
Equity	$ 50,000	$ 40,000
Mortgage	$ 100,000	$185,000

RESULT: Tax is due on $10,000 of cash boot taken.

Example 3: Exchanger goes down in value, across in equity, and down in mortgage

	RELINQUISHED	**REPLACEMENT**
Value	$150,000	$125,000
Equity	$ 50,000	$ 50,000
Mortgage	$100,000	$ 75,000

RESULT: Tax is due on the $25,000 of mortgage boot received.

Here are some of the key requirements for completing the exchange properly:

45-Day Rule: The exchanger must identify the potential replacement properties within the first 45 days of the 180 day exchange period. The time limits begin to run on the date the exchanger transfers the first relinquished property to the buyer.

▶ **NOTE**

There is NO EXTENSION of these deadlines for Saturdays, Sundays, or holidays.

Property Identification:

1. must be delivered to a party in the exchange that is not a disqualified party (i.e., to the qualified intermediary).
2. must be in writing and signed by the exchanger.
3. must be unambiguous (site specific).
4. can be revoked within the 45 days, but the revocation must follow steps 1 through 4.

But how many replacement properties is the exchanger allowed to identify?

More than one potential replacement property can be identified as long as you satisfy one of these rules:

1. **The Three Property Rule:** You may identify up to three properties regardless of their market values. All identified properties are not required to be purchased to satisfy the exchange, only the amount needed to satisfy the value requirement.
2. **The 200% Rule:** Any number of properties may be identified as long as the aggregate fair market value (FMV) of all replacement properties does not exceed 200% of the aggregate fair market value of all of the relinquished properties as of the initial transfer date. All identified properties are not required to be purchased to satisfy the exchange, only the amount needed to satisfy the value requirement.
3. **The 95% Rule:** Any number of replacement properties may be identified if the fair market value of the properties actually received by the end of the exchange period is at least 95% of the aggregate fair market value (FMV) of all the potential replacement properties identified. In other words, 95% (or all) of the properties identified must be purchased or the entire exchange is invalid.

What Happens if We Do NOT Complete the Exchange as Planned?

Surprisingly, about 20% of all planned 1031 exchanges ARE NOT completed! Most failures to complete occur because the exchanger fails to correctly identify the replacement properties in a timely manner. If you cannot identify the replacement properties within 45 days, it is a sale! No extension of the 45-day clock is permitted, the exchange is denied, and it's a taxable event.

▶ NOTE

As an IPS assisting your investors with their exchanges, here are a couple of ways you can help them PLAN AHEAD to avoid having their exchange fail due to improper identification:

---

1. They can delay the close of escrow on the relinquished property to gain more time to find a replacement property. You should write a specific contingency into the sales agreement to facilitate a delay if needed. Ask for an additional 30 days or more to close. The 45-day clock doesn't begin until close of escrow on this first transaction.

2. They can get into contract to purchase the replacement property BEFORE they sell the relinquished property! This obviates the 45-day crunch period and can be accomplished much more often than not if you plan ahead and begin your search early enough.

What Are YOUR Exit Strategies?

When you have completed building your real estate empire and are ready to reap the fruits of your labor, many of you will happily remain in the driver's seat continuing to manage your rental properties and businesses, while others of you will be ready to shift to a more passive phase in which you merely want to enjoy your retirement with no continuing interest in managing your properties. Whichever way you are thinking, the earlier you determine your strategy, the easier the transition will likely be.

For those of you who are planning to turn your investments over to your children or family, I hope you have not waited until this time to tell them about your plan for their assuming control of the reins on the old property sled. If you really want them to have the advantage of running the business you've built, get them involved as early as you can so that they have time to appreciate the realities and the benefits of continuing the business and so that you have time to teach them how to operate the business. If you do not, they will have undoubtedly made their own plans for the future which won't include continuing with your real estate interests, and they likely will only want to see the properties sold and converted to assets they can use as soon as possible.

If your family-owned properties are held by a family trust in which you are the trustee, you can easily designate your children as successor trustees who assume management responsibility upon your demise or in the event you become disabled. This will thereby provide a seamless transfer of control and avoid probate or tax payments because the trust merely continues and only the trustee changes. If you have not already done so, discuss the best way to establish such a structure with your CPA or tax advisor.

If your plan is to become a passive recipient of the income from your rental property business, there are several ways you can accomplish this.

Installment Sales

You can sell your properties individually—or en masse—by creating a single or a series of installment sales. In an installment sale you typically carry back the financing (or part of it) secured by notes, trust deeds, or mortgages on the properties and receive payments on those mortgages over a period of time, say 20 years. Because installment sales allow sellers to defer recognition of gains on the sale of a business or real estate to the tax year in which the related sale proceeds are received, you effectively spread out paying taxes on the new mortgage payments over the 20 year period. The actual time period for repayment is completely negotiable between buyer and seller. An installment sale may be just the right answer for you.

What can go wrong with an installment sale? Generally, not much! The most common hiccups are:

1. When the buyer has some kind of financial catastrophe and cannot complete the payments as agreed. If they cannot resolve

the issue, the seller's remedy is to foreclose and take the property back. This may not represent a significant loss, only an annoying setback with the seller needing to start over with the installment sale process.

2. Sometimes, it's difficult to find the right buyer because buyers often want to complete a 1031 exchange out of another property they are relinquishing and into your property using all cash proceeds, which they must spend now, not over 20 years. Happily, this problem can be easily overcome by utilizing a structured sale to correct the buyer-seller mismatch.

What IS a Structured Sale?

A structured sale (also called an ensured installment sale) can be used for the sale of either a business or real property, and it essentially combines the tax deferral benefits of an installment sale with the surety of a structured annuity to ensure that taxes are paid as funds are received rather than due upon sale. The potential problem of the shaky buyer isn't a factor either because the seller's payment stream comes from an insurance company that regularly issues and pays annuity installments.

The buyer completes his 1031 exchange and immediately receives title to the property, and his funds are directed to the insurance company providing the annuity to the seller who can have the payment of the annuity structured any way he likes. Neither buyer nor seller incurs an expense for the creation of the annuity; the structured settlement specialist who implements the transaction is paid directly by the life insurance company that writes the annuity.

▶ NOTE

Another use for the structured sale is as a backup plan for a seller who cannot find a replacement property to complete his 1031 tax-deferred exchange. If he has closed on his relinquished property but has no replacement property identified, he can still accomplish an installment sale using a structured sale. When you consider that 20% of all 1031 exchanges FAIL, perhaps the low-cost insurance of setting up a structured sale is a worthwhile ounce of prevention? A knowledgeable IPS will make sure his exchanger knows about this option! Of course, the exchanger should discuss this procedure with his CPA or tax advisor!

Recommended Reading List

1. *The 16% Solution* by Joel Moskowitz

CHAPTER SEVEN

Should Your Investment Strategy Include Taking On Partners?

The question of taking on partners to help in your business is an age-old one, and the answer is always, "It depends...." It depends primarily upon what kind of help you need to complete your business objectives and whether adding that help is best accomplished by hiring assistants or by adding partners who will share in the workload and ownership of your business enterprise.

There Are Many Reasons We Might Entertain Taking On Partners

Oftentimes, we seek partners because we do not have all the skills or experience required to accomplish our objectives by ourselves. If we team up with others who can provide the complementary skills we lack, we can all benefit from such a union.

One of the major reasons new business owners buy franchises is to learn the trade from partners who have the needed expertise and track record to show them how to shortcut the process of learning how to do it the hard way. Successful franchisees are able to follow the franchisor's exact, proven procedures to minimize the learning curve attendant to all new businesses.

We may also want to consider partnering if we are constrained by a lack of available time or funds needed to complete the business' workload by ourselves. Sharing the workload, expanding the available funding to complete the project in better fashion, or completing it sooner, could directly improve the chances of obtaining a successful completion.

As we discussed in Chapter Three: Understanding Investment Properties, it's important that we carefully examine exactly what we want our real estate investment business to do for us and to commit that plan to writing to insure that the path we choose to pursue is clearly articulated. Is your plan one you can accomplish alone or will adding partners improve both your likelihood of success and accelerate your timetable? Will the addition of partners possibly facilitate enlarging the scope, complexity, growth, and earnings of your business while compressing the timeframe for growing your investment portfolio?

If it's urgent that YOU be in complete control of your investment business, you will undoubtedly be better served by figuring out how you can afford to hire assistants to help you run the business. That way, if the nature of the business or the tasks to be done change, you can simply hire more or different assistants. If the only help you need is financial contribution, there are several ways you can remain in control of the business' day-to-day operations while partnering with other investors.

While adding partners can be undertaken using several different organizational structures, you will always have the obligation of sharing either the workload or the business' profits and ownership with those partners.

Before we examine some of the particular types of partnership structures you as a real estate investor could consider implementing, let's consider the possibility of selecting partners who you already know...and trust!

Investing with Family Members—Will It Work for YOU?

There are some compelling reasons to consider investing with members of your family...but it may not work well for everyone. What should you consider before embarking on a family-operated investment project?

1. One of the best reasons to invest with other family members—or any other partner[6], for that matter—is to be able to do projects together that you might be unable to do alone or perhaps could not do as easily or as well alone.
    a. You can combine your financial, physical, and time resources to control more top-line real estate, accomplish more work or

[6] The term "partner" is used generically here. Your group can be an LLC, a corporation, or any other entity recommended by your tax professional or business or estate planning attorney.

do it quicker, and enjoy the advantage of having a "partner" to brainstorm solutions to problems and opportunities with.

b. Using family members as investment partners can be a very comfortable way to select a partner, for the obvious reason that (normally) you already know each other well, have an existing relationship, and (if it's a good one) have a good basis for trust and confidence in one another.

2. Family partnerships have the advantage that they tend to survive the ups-and-downs you'll encounter in your investment projects because you're less likely to dissolve a relationship with someone who will remain a member of the family when the project is done. Having abundance mentality and a bit of patience will help ensure a partnership's longevity and thereby contribute to your venture's success.

3. Before starting a family investment partnership or group, consider what your common investment objectives are as a family.

   a. Are you jointly interested in building wealth by owning properties which will provide cash flow or equity growth? Do you all have similar plans and timeframes in mind to hold, trade, or sell these properties?

      Then what? 1031 tax-deferred exchanges? Together or separately? In other words, what is your exit strategy? If you DO plan to dissolve the entity that holds title to the properties, it's important that you consider exactly how the title is held because should you decide to go your separate ways and utilize separate, individual 1031 exchanges to exit the properties, you must be able to maintain the ownership entity throughout the exchange, e.g., the entity that relinquishes the present property must be exactly the same entity that purchases the replacement property. (See Chapter Six: How Do You Build And Manage a Real Estate Portfolio Successfully? for discussion of 1031 tax-deferred exchanges.)

   b. Perhaps you're more interested in jointly owning family vacation properties to use exclusively yourselves or to rent and use between short-term, vacationing tenants? This can be a good basis for a family partnership although it may sometimes not produce the best return on investment.

c. What are the resources each of you will contribute? Will all of you participate equally in management of the asset? Will all of you participate equally financially? How will you share in enjoyment of the property for personal use?

   It's important to be certain all partners are aware of and comfortable with the other partner's expected contributions and their anticipated rewards to avoid later misunderstandings.

4. Clearly, it's imperative that all partners in ANY business venture must be on the same page concerning the project's specific goals in order to succeed...and to do so without unnecessary strife!

   a. How do we guarantee that our objectives are the same?

      WE MUST WRITE THEM DOWN (Yes, even with dear old Uncle Billy. If Uncle Billy suddenly contracts amnesia or is hit by a train, we must know in advance how to handle this tragedy for the sake of his other partners and his heirs. That means knowing what the plan was in reasonable detail so that all parties' wishes are observed, including Uncle Billy's.)

      It may be a good idea to consider having key man insurance to provide for an unexpected incapacity of one or more of the decision makers or leaders of your enterprise. If you think this may be worth considering, contact your insurance agent and learn what your options are.

   b. The best way to set up the venture for a successful outcome is to agree on what a successful outcome looks like—for everyone!

   c. We must decide how our partnership BEGINS, how it is CONDUCTED while in operation, and how it ENDS (if it does).

   d. Define the partnership's purpose, the probable start date, the expected duration, the funding requirements of each partner, as well as who will do what and when will it be done. How will the proceeds of the partners be distributed at the termination of the venture or the partnership? If additional interim funding is required of the partners, how will that be handled?

e. However formally or informally you decide to create the written description of your partnership, just do it! It will assure that you start by getting everyone committed to the same plan. That alone will serve you very well in the investment legacy you create for future generations of your family!

f. Be sure to plan on how you will keep all partners advised of business details, plans, and progress. Will you conduct meetings with the participants periodically to dispense information and to charter assignments?

   Who will be responsible for managing the finances, accounting, and conducting the day-to-day business of your enterprise? Will any of the participants receive a salary or wages for task work? Will you hire staff? Will travel be required by any of the participants, and if so, has the travel cost been anticipated and added to your budget?

   How do all the members obtain visibility of the operations and concurrence in the ongoing tasks and obligations that each must perform?

▶ NOTE

Your choice of partnership structure may require that you conduct meetings, record minutes of those meetings, and observe proper meeting protocols, especially if you need to provide evidence of proper operation to conform with corporate legal requirements. Discuss the record keeping and voting requirements with your advisors when establishing your asset protection entity structure or structures.

Many partnerships that fail do so because of misunderstandings and poor communication between the principals. Joining forces can provide a great advantage for the participants, but failure to communicate can lead to disenchantment and may obscure the benefits of the association. If you don't know what your partner is doing or why he's doing it, it's sometimes hard to simply operate on blind faith and hope for the best. More importantly, it's not a strategy that's calculated to engender confidence and well-being.

If you've discovered compelling reasons to band together to start a new venture to begin with, your chances of success will absolutely DEPEND upon good communication between the parties and agreement upon the tasks and methods of operation you will employ together.

Some Examples of Successful Family Investment Groups

What does a successful family investment partnership look like?

We've had several family investment groups within our Real Estate Guys Radio™ Investor Mentoring Club, including the families of both Robert Helms and Russell Gray—the club's founders and the authors of Equity Happens. But just as you'd suspect, some families thrive on family partnerships, while others can't even conceive of that possibility.

1. My brother Bill and I created a partnership to buy investment properties in about 1970. Prior to that time, we each owned our own homes in Northern California and had operated some single-family rentals. We bought several properties together including a medical-dental office building, a 50-unit apartment building, and a couple of smaller Victorian apartments in downtown San Jose which we operated together. We finally dissolved this partnership that had endured for over 30 years because we sold the last property we owned jointly and we each pursued other avenues with our children and other family members.

   This partnership operated smoothly during its tenure because both families made significant contributions to its operation. We each contributed capital, management expertise, time, and energy, and continually collaborated on solving the problems that cropped up over time. The partnership was a very successful operation that performed well.

   Yet, if we were starting that partnership again today, we'd be sure to make a few changes. The major difference would first be to establish a more beneficial entity structure to afford us better liability and asset protection and tax benefits to help us enjoy even more success.

2. In Chapter Two: Lessons Learned From my First Transaction as an IPS, I described meeting some old salts who had also joined the new real estate firm to work as IPSs. I was able to receive much-needed coaching and a lot of other help from this group.

One of those gentlemen later became my partner in owning and operating a small, local brokerage. Jerry also became Robert Helms' first broker, and Robert recalls his introduction to the office. Jerry showed him around, showed him his desk, introduced him to the other agents, and then explained that Robert shouldn't expect to spend much time there, because no one in the office was going to buy anything from him. All Robert's customers would be found OUTSIDE of the office! Welcome to Cambridge Properties and your new real estate career, Robert!

Jerry and I had a solid, enjoyable partnership. We played golf two days per week, meeting before the local municipal course was open for business. We walked the course, carried our bags, discussed our business activities, finished 18 holes, paid to play on the way out, arriving at the office by 9:30 AM ready for the day's activities. I'm happy to say that almost 30 years later, Robert and I both still have a great relationship with Jerry, who is a classy guy and a dependable business partner.

3. When Robert first joined Jerry and me at Cambridge Properties in 1987, we sold new homes for a builder in Cupertino, California. The builder-developers were four brothers whose father was a wealthy Hong Kong developer. The brothers attended four different universities in the U.S., then formed their construction company with advice and financial help from their father. Unlike most small builders, they were well-financed and paid cash for land and materials, allowing them to compete very successfully. They hired good architects and feng shui consultants and produced many high-end homes and subdivisions that were well accepted by the homebuying public.

   I think a major reason their partnership thrived was that they divided their duties and responsibilities, researched the marketplace well, and enjoyed the advantages of being a family first and a business second. They also utilized their family finances for the benefit of all. Their father did not simply give them the money to open their homebuilding business; he instead, helped them start the new business, but it was their responsibility to operate it successfully and profitably.

One of the lessons we learned from this group was that their thinking was different than most of the American contractors they competed with, and it had nothing to do with their formal education. They were from a wealthy Chinese family, and they definitely looked at things on a much longer timeframe than most of their U.S. counterparts. Specifically, they looked at family wealth preservation from a generational viewpoint, treasuring education and good financial stewardship. The homes they built also reflected their family values, because every model was designed to house three generations of family members.

4. Robert and I were real estate partners representing buyers and sellers for 18 years before Robert decided to concentrate on developing new investment properties by syndicating with other investors. Prior to joining Cambridge Properties, Robert managed a 50-unit family-owned apartment building. He inherited the manager's job from his grandfather, and eventually the job was passed on to his cousin. Robert was reasonably well prepared both for a career in real estate investing and for operating in a family business environment. I firmly believe that Robert and I were able to work side-by-side because we gave each other plenty of space and a lot of mutual respect in our daily work environment. We both contributed to our success as partners, and it was a very satisfying relationship.

5. Robert also went into partnership with one of his college buddies operating a frozen yogurt shop, and they earned some of the money needed to open it by helping me do a partial renovation to an old family owned Victorian apartment building. Imagine scraping two-inch sections of ancient wallpaper from 12 - 14 foot walls (by hand, of course) for several weeks to raise some of the capital they needed…so they could become yogurt yerks!

   Before beginning their joint venture, they had what Robert calls "the talk." They were crystal clear about their relationship being much more important than the partnership itself and vowed that their friendship would prevail. The result? After a few seasons of "making great money in the summer" and then "putting it all back in the winter," they decided to retire from yogurting...and they are still great friends 30 years later! The partnership was a success, the business venture not so much!

But This Family Wisely Opted not to Become Partners

Robert and I also met four other brothers whose parents died, and they asked us to sell their parent's home in San Jose. Robert suggested that the home would produce a much higher price if they invested a little work and time to update it before selling. The brother who was the executor declined, stating that the family history clearly indicated that he would be the only one willing to work to achieve the needed improvements, but all would insist on equal division of the sales proceeds. A family partnership was not a good solution in this case. Although they could have made more money, they didn't think it was worth the hassle of dealing with non-cooperative siblings. Clearly, they knew each other well!

The Pros and Cons of Investing with your Family

What are the pros and cons of forming a family investment group?

Some of the Pros to Consider

1. Combining your resources and assets to achieve greater results or to compress timeframes.
2. Capitalizing and building on already established relationships with people who know you, trust you, and care about you. Your aunt may be a good candidate to invest in your project using her self-directed IRA because of your relationship. She can be a direct investment partner or she could provide loans which can be secured by the properties.
3. WRITE DOWN YOUR PLAN. Don't expect it to be perfect, but writing it will cause you to think and plan more carefully. As individuals grow and improve and new opportunities present themselves, allow for changes...but be sure to discuss and agree to incorporate them. Before finalizing your agreement, you definitely want to consult your CPA, your real estate attorney and your estate planning attorney for their advice. Even if you have a great plan for the OPERATION of the business, the STRUCTURE of your group will be important for both liability and asset protection and maximizing tax benefits.

Not only can you create a better estate to leave your family, you can structure more effective ways to pass that inheritance to your family, and be assured that they will know what to do with it. Their early involvement in the family business can prepare them to utilize the inheritance effectively for the benefit of themselves and their own future inheritors. It's also important to structure your family trusts and entities to protect your hard-earned assets.

4. Just as with a new job, if your family are experienced investors, you can often "borrow" or leverage the family credibility to accelerate your investment prowess and opportunities.

Some of the Cons to Consider

If you love your aunt, but not so much your cousin, maybe you should partner with your aunt! A family member needs to ADD to the investment partnership, not DETRACT from it. Being family is great, it's just not sufficient as a reason to become partners. If your cousin is not someone you'd choose as a partner, pick another cousin or your aunt!

1. Is your family partner fully aware of the realities of investing in real estate? If not, are they willing to let you lead them? It's imperative that you come to a common understanding about the purpose, scope, and operation of your family investment business.
2. Many people are very reluctant to discuss or conduct ANY business with other family members. So be it!

Make a list of the pros and cons for the property and partnership you wish to pursue. BE BRUTALLY HONEST about your willingness to undertake it and consider what safeguards, if any, will improve your chances of success. I have a statement about relationship with others that I like to revisit EVERY TIME I contemplate a new joint venture or project. It goes like this:

"The truth about the relationship is available to you at the beginning of the relationship—if you will have the courage to look carefully at what you know about the person, about yourself, and about your objective..." So, I'm recommending that you look very closely at the potential partner before consummating the agreement. In other words, take off your rose-colored glasses (that you are wearing because you really want this to work), and look carefully at what your references and research tell you! It is often much easier to start a new partnership than it is to disentangle yourself from an unsatisfactory one.

I have personally enjoyed great success working with and investing with my family, so I know it works well for us. I wish you the same success if you determine that the pros of working together outweigh the cons.

If Not Family Partners, Then Who DO I Partner With?

If you are an IPS or working to become an IPS, consider the possibility of working with and training other IPS agents to combine your efforts and theirs to emphasize your investment property business. Most new agents do not "speak income" at all—let alone fluently—but that can be solved by education, if they are motivated. Envision your becoming part of a go-to team that aggressively tackles the investor marketplace in your town. Since there is very little competition for this business, you can set the standard for providing much needed assistance to the investors in your community. You can create a strong and welcome presence as the go-to team of choice. Whether you form a formal partnership or merely decide to collaborate to your mutual advantage, you are likely to produce a strong business segment that the investment community will welcome because, up to this point, no one else has even thought about doing that.

Selecting the Best Partnership Structure for Your Business

There are many choices available to anyone who wants to start a new business entity. You can simply operate by yourself as a sole proprietor, or opt to form a corporation in the state where you reside, or elsewhere, which may entail any number of operations from a small family business, to a multifaceted manufacturing organization employing numerous employees, in multiple locations. The number of options available is your first clue that this is not a simple process. It will require study and the assistance of experienced counsel to select an appropriate entity or entities that provide the best balance between asset protection, tax treatment, and ease of operating the business.

All businesses have the potential for liability in delivering the goods or services they provide, so attention must be paid to minimizing the liabilities and the attendant risk of lawsuits that can jeopardize your business' profits. Your first and primary line of defense is to have general comprehensive business insurance coverage for general liability protection against accidents or mishaps and, if available, errors and omissions insurance to protect you from inadvertent mistakes or negligence claims.

Limited Partnerships

A limited partnership will be comprised of a general partner as well as one or more limited partners who unite to conduct a business together. The general partner is responsible for the day-to-day operation of the business' activities, and is liable for its conduct, as well as its ongoing expenditures and obligations. The limited partners, who are not active in management, are not liable for the debts of the partnership beyond the investment monies they contribute to fund the business' operations initially. Of course, limited partners do participate in the flow of income and expenses derived from the limited partnership's business.

Limited partnerships do provide a structure that can work well for the manager who must be in control of operations and key decisions, which is the general partner's role.

It is also quite common for investors who have utilized all their available funds to seek new financial partners who want to take advantage of that investor's experience and ability to be involved in deal flow. The new financial partners get to participate in the transaction the investor locates, contracts and manages, thereby earning a share of the returns the project generates. These investor groups can take the form of partnerships or even joint ventures, but are most commonly done with syndications using appropriate entity structures to safeguard the syndication's assets. It is essential that the syndicator engage the services of a securities lawyer to assist in forming the entity structuring and to review the compensation and distribution of profits to the members to ensure that the syndication is in conformance with government security regulations.

How Do You Select The RIGHT Partner?

No matter what kind of partnership you elect to use, the MOST important thing you must do before you agree-to-agree to become partners is to be completely realistic about the consequences of the intended relationship with the prospective partner. I suggest that while a handshake may be adequate to signal your intent to cooperate, a handshake is no substitute for research regarding the suitability of that partner as a person you are ready to share risk and profits with, perhaps over a relatively long-term period.

Moreover, if you do decide to go ahead and form the partnership, it's critical that you clearly define who is doing what for whom, so your next requisite step is to:

1. Write down the details of how you expect this partnership to function over the course of its life, so that you have a clear agreement about how, when, and where the partnership will conduct its business.
2. How will it begin? What are the roles and responsibilities of its members? Will it operate from a central physical location, or will each member perform his duties independently, and from his own office?
3. How will it function during its normal and routine operations? What are the regular tasks to be performed by each partner? Who is the partnership's manager, and how are they compensated? Is regular travel required of the manager, and has that travel been budgeted? How will you communicate the milestones and achievements of the partnership to its members?

▶ NOTE

If something happens to the partnership's manager which precludes his ability to continue to manage the business' activities, will one of the other partners be sufficiently skilled and be able to step in and manage in his place? If not, does the partnership have sufficient budget or assets to hire an outside replacement manager? This can become a significant issue if the manager was not receiving a promote fee, expense reimbursements, or other compensation from the business, and you are now unable to find someone to take his place without their receiving either some form of ownership or income.

---

4. At the conclusion of the partnership's project(s), how will the partnership terminate? Are the partnership properties to be sold? Are the properties to be refinanced and held for cash flow or equity

growth? What is the planned exit strategy? If sold, is the formula for returning the investor's contributions clearly understood by each partner? Has the profit sharing formula between the investors and the manager been clearly identified? Has the manager completed and distributed the final accounting to the members or provided for a CPA firm to do so?

To summarize, it's imperative that the partners are in agreement on exactly how the partnership will BEGIN, how it will OPERATE, and how it will END (if indeed, it does). I strongly recommend that once you have determined the direction you want to take, you then engage the services of a CPA, tax attorney, or asset protection attorney to ensure that you choose the best entity structure to achieve your goals while providing asset protection and liability coverage to safeguard your investments.

Syndications

In Chapter Six: Building Your Real Estate Portfolio, we discussed the opportunity to create or enlarge the scope of your real estate projects by utilizing your investment skills to find deals that lend themselves to participation with partners. While any number of entity structures could be utilized to accomplish working with partners, private syndications allow you to customize your project to provide workable outcomes and exit strategies for your investors, most of whom will passively invest their money, but not their time or skills. The vision, the design, and the responsibility for completion of the project normally rest with you, the syndicator.

▶ NOTE

CAUTION: Be aware that whenever you accept and manage investor funds with an expectation of a return on that investment, you are dealing with a security, and you must comply with all federal and state security laws. Be sure to engage the services of an attorney who is familiar with securities regulations to ensure that your syndication complies with all appropriate regulations.

If you are an IPS contemplating becoming a syndicator, there are various ways you might accomplish this, and how you start is probably more dependent upon your experience as an investor than any other factor. If you're sufficiently experienced to be able to find a credible deal, create the project's organization and charter, design what is to be done, and determine who will do it, what it will cost, what the newly transformed property will look like in addition to showing your investors an attractive enough return on investment for them to be willing to fund your project, you can do this now if you have the confidence to undertake it.

If you are not yet that experienced, your best opportunity to learn the necessary skills is probably to team up with an experienced syndicator investor as a passive investor yourself, so that you are close enough to see how a syndication is done. Ideally, you want to learn to be part of a team or learn enough to create your own team. If you are in at the early stages, you can be helping your sponsor find the deal, creating the project's vision, and helping with as many phases of the operation as you can so that you learn as much as possible. Whether you do future projects alone or with others, you'll want to learn to contribute as much as you can and learn how all the work is done from creating the physical project, to obtaining the permits necessary for its completion, to writing the executive summary that explains your offering to investors, to finding potential investors and presenting the opportunity to them.

Private Syndications

The Real Estate Guys™ provide excellent training for syndicators in their Secrets of Successful Syndication seminar, which is offered two or three times a year in varying locations throughout the U.S. Go to their website at www.RealEstateGuysRadio.com and click on *Events*, then select *Secrets of Successful Syndication* for details and schedules.

Once you have acquired sufficient experience and ability, you can create private syndications which allow other investors to participate with you in the investment vehicles you design. This is often a great way to increase your next project's size and complexity, and to begin to attract happy investors who want to do it again!

Syndications can readily accelerate the rate at which you can grow your business by combining the skills you have or will learn with the resources of other participants to help expand both the scale and pace of your business activity and acumen while providing your investors opportunities they would not be able to realize by themselves.

One of the more important attributes of participating in a private investment vehicle is that it is indeed PRIVATE. The sponsor, operator, or syndicator may indeed be a visible participant, but the passive investor members are not, so they remain invisible to the general public, which most investors will be happy about.

Successful syndicators typically begin their syndication careers by finding and structuring deals or projects that require them to create or stretch their database of investors to raise enough funds to complete that project. Because their skillset normally includes finding deals—but not raising money from investors—they absolutely believe that finding deals is easy, but finding investor monies is much harder...and they're right. At that stage of their career, it is harder for them to find investor money than it is to find new deals.

But fast forward a few deals, or a few years, and those same syndicators will have learned that their situation has changed. If they have indeed put together deals that have been successful and have provided attractive returns to those investors, they are now finding that their happy investors don't WANT them to return their money (which has now accumulated some friends along the way). They are quite HAPPY with the returns and want to keep their money working!

As they compile their track record of success and more experience envisioning and creating successful deals for their investors to participate in, these syndicators now have no problem raising more money. Their problem becomes keeping adequate deal flow available for their investors! Most of these syndicators will find themselves searching multiple marketplaces to find new opportunities for their investors. The most successful syndicators virtually have investors and investor money waiting in line to fund their next deal.

So the primary objective of a successful syndicator is to consistently produce successful projects that deliver good returns, thereby building a reputation for delivering what they've promised. This is what produces a waiting line of new investors, eager to participate in your next deal.

It's imperative that in growing your business and your reputation you not lose sight of the very real possibility that your next deal could go south and end up NOT delivering the results you hoped for. Even with the best possible planning, deals don't always work exactly as you envisioned or planned them. Your project can encounter unforeseen events. (Does the market crash of 2008 come to mind?) which fundamentally change your ability to survive an unexpected catastrophe. If you engage in real estate investing for a long enough period of time, the likelihood of a failed project looms larger. Exemplary stewardship of your investor's money is always needed, but that can sometimes be insufficient to preserve the outcome you were seeking.

Realizing that such a possibility can occur should give you pause to consider the significance of how such a disaster will affect each of your investors. It's much harder for your investor to accept a business loss when that investor has imprudently invested more than he could afford to lose. The earlier a syndicator realizes that it is unwise to accept just anyone who has the necessary funds, the better he will be able to comfortably choose the right investors for his projects, and build a long-term client list of happy repeat investors. It IS possible for a project to fail, without ending your career as a syndicator and without ending your client's appetite for additional investment opportunities. While no one will be happy about a project's poor performance, it's important that we realize it can happen, and it's important that we carefully study the reasons for the failure. In other words, we want to "get the lessons" to help us avoid repeating the mistakes.

Projects do fail sometimes, but the world of investment opportunities continues to attract participants, and often causes us to approach new opportunities with renewed vigor. As we learn the lessons entailed, it is our job to put our new discoveries back to work and to become better at what we do.

It will become critically important that you have set up your syndication correctly to ensure compliance with securities regulations if your project fails and your investors suffer financial losses. They can ask for their money back, and you will need to show that the venture was properly registered, or was exempt from registration, and that the opportunity you presented to them was clearly described in terms of both the benefits anticipated and the risks attendant to the investment. It is incumbent upon the syndicator to provide all the information a prudent investor would want to know before deciding to invest with you. If your offerings originate within the United States, you will need to file with both the Securities and Exchange Commission (SEC) and every state in which you contact potential investors detailing the specific exemption(s) that apply. Your securities attorney can provide the details and guidance you need.

My experience is that most syndicators are extremely conscientious about representing their project's opportunities for return on investment accurately and responsibly, just as they are dedicated to providing careful management of their project's assets. Syndication investors are definitely best served by receiving projections of earnings that are under-promised and over-delivered. Remember, each of us has only one reputation, and our ability to bounce back from adversity and succeed long-term depends on safeguarding it, incorporating the lessons learned, and working to become more accomplished.

Should You Invest in Your Own Syndication?

One of the questions your investors are likely to ask is, "Are you invested in the project yourself?" While there is no one correct answer to this question that will ensure 100% participation by prospective investors, you can be sure the average investor would be much happier knowing that YOU are both a fan AND supporter of your own project! Syndication details are normally private, but syndicators routinely invest somewhere between 5 to 20% of the total raise themselves, and it's easy to see why investors are more comfortable investing alongside their syndication sponsor, especially when they have evidence that:

1. The sponsor has a history of investing in his own syndicated projects.
2. The sponsor is also depending on a successful outcome for the project in order to be paid himself.
3. Investors have a preferred return. While there are no laws or rules controlling exactly how the profits are shared between the syndicator and rest of a project's investors upon completion, a sound strategy for profit distribution will usually begin by giving the investors a preferred return which they receive before the sponsor is paid his share, excluding returns on the syndicator's personal cash contribution.

What Are Some Creative Ways to Structure Private Syndications?

Syndicate a Property You Already Own

One method of finding a great deal can be creating a syndication for a property (or group of properties) that you or one of your investors already owns! Using a property you already own, or one that can be readily controlled by you or your group, allows you more time to structure and perform the agreements and conditions of the purchase contract, while you obtain commitments from your investors, contractors, municipalities involved, etc. You will have more time to:

1. Do your due diligence and inspections up front
2. Obtain written bids for work required and timetables to complete
3. Control parameters and timing of 1031 exchanges, if applicable
4. Establish workable timeframes for organization and completion of projects
5. Utilize pertinent data and experience that ownership provides
6. Thoroughly research the marketplace you're already familiar with
7. Add additional units, update amenities, and create higher value

Structure a Joint Venture with Another Property Owner

You need not own the land yourself if you can structure a joint venture with a landowner who essentially partners with the syndication to complete whatever vision you can jointly agree on. The landowner contributes the property, and the syndicator and his investor partners provide the funds and management necessary to complete the project. Obviously, you'll need to devise an equitable division of the profits realized to make this a win-win for all the participants.

Create an Exploratory Fund

If you do not immediately have a viable project in hand, you may wish to form an exploratory fund to buy targets of opportunity you find in specific marketplaces, and you may certainly still be able to create an offering that will interest real estate investors. Having cash in hand (or nearly in hand) will allow you to negotiate with sellers from a position of strength.

Having sufficient experience and expertise in a particular market segment—perhaps one that you have worked in previously—will allow you to demonstrate your understanding of the opportunity, and why you think the likelihood of success is great enough to warrant investor's participation. You can be more selective and competitive pursuing the projects you choose to undertake, when you work with cash.

The trade-off of having a cash fund is that you will want to deploy it as soon as practicable in order not to delay and thereby dilute your investor's returns any longer than necessary. Alternatively, you can have a pledge from your investors to fund upon demand when you have found and contracted to purchase the properties. However, such a strategy will require that the investors can be relied on to fund upon demand. That's why it's a trade-off between having the cash in hand and being able to execute when you find the property, however long that takes, versus being able to execute immediately, thereby reducing the amount of time the investor's funds are sitting idle. That is if they all fund their pledges upon demand!

Projects such as this which are funded before selecting a particular property to purchase are often called blind pool investments, because you won't be able to show your investor participants a detailed financial analysis, and they must rely solely upon your experience and expertise in selecting appropriate properties to purchase. Obviously, you will need to demonstrate a successful track record as a syndicator to attract investors to participate in your exploratory fund opportunities.

So...Do You Take On Partners or Not?

The choice of whether to take on partners is not a simple one, and you may be influenced by your prior successes or failures with other partnerships, but it's certainly worth considering when the benefits of combining your energies and efforts with others offers the promise of handling bigger and better projects that can propel your career forward.

Recommended Reading List

1. *How to Use Limited Liability Companies and Limited Partnerships* by Garrett Sutton and Cindie Geddes

2. *Real Estate Blind Pools* by Douglas Slain, M.A., J.D.

Other Resources

The Real Estate Guys™ seminar Secrets of Successful Syndication is presented several times a year in varying locations. For more information, go to www.RealEstateGuysRadio.com and click on *Events*.

CHAPTER EIGHT

Using IRAs to Buy Investment Real Estate

Apparently, one of the best-kept secrets in America is that you can use your self-directed IRAs (SDIRAs) to buy investment properties. In fact, those IRA funds are intended to be used only for investment purposes! So, yes, you may definitely use your SDIRA to buy investment properties!

So why do I call it a secret? Because few investors, and even fewer real estate agents, are aware of the power of utilizing IRAs to accelerate the acquisition of investment properties into their portfolios. And for those IRA owners who aren't interested in owning more properties, they also have the option to lend funds from their IRA accounts to other investors or homebuyers and realize substantial returns on those investments, utilizing a trust deed or mortgage on the property as the security for the loan.

And, they have the option of using their IRA funds to purchase precious metals, or tax lien certificates, tax deed sales, and much, much more.

To effectively utilize your self-directed IRA, you definitely need to understand the rules; but most IRAs are held captive by the big Wall Street firms that would have you and your investor clients believe that your options are very limited and that it's completely unsafe for you to take responsibility for engaging in other vehicles outside their stocks, bonds, and mutual fund accounts—*which are the only things they have to sell you!* Many investment firms work hard to dissuade you from taking over the investment reins by emphasizing the FUD principle (instilling you with Fear, Uncertainty, and Doubt regarding your ability to make decisions without their guidance). This is because these large financial institutions have little incentive to recommend something other than stocks, bonds, or mutual funds which bring in extremely profitable commission and fees for them.

Because your IRA is a retirement vehicle, there are many IRS rules controlling what is or isn't allowed, but both you and your investors are capable of understanding them, and your IRA custodian[7] can and will help you follow the IRS guidelines. Your IRA custodian cannot and will not give you investment advice or suggest where you should invest, but they will tell you what is or isn't permitted. Don't let your stockbroker talk you out of learning whether the opportunities available to you are worthwhile. This is YOUR retirement money, not theirs, and you have a wide variety of choices available to you when investing your self-directed IRA funds.

It's not surprising that most IRA owners are unaware that they can (or that it may be in their interest to) to self-direct the investments that they make with their IRA funds, since those IRA owners have very few advocates helping them learn about the benefits of self-directing their IRAs. You might expect that they would receive help from the real estate agents who specialize in helping them buy, sell, or exchange their investment properties, but, alas, there are actually very few of those agents in existence, and fewer yet who know anything about using IRAs to purchase real estate, so almost no help is forthcoming from that sector.

The IRA custodian executes transactions on behalf of the client, keeps all necessary and appropriate records of all actions undertaken in the custodial capacity, and files any reports, such as statements and tax notices required either by the custodial agreement or the law. The custodian is responsible for distributing the IRA's assets in accordance with the client's instructions and filing the appropriate paperwork. An IRA custodian is not required to give investment or legal advice, so it is the responsibility of the client to make sure that all directions given to the custodian are compliant with the IRS code.

The assets of an IRA may be invested in a wide variety of securities and other financial instruments. Regulations prohibit the investment of IRA assets in collectibles such as art and rare coins and in life insurance, but other investments such as real estate, franchises, mortgages, and tax

---

[7] An IRA custodian is typically a financial institution, such as a bank or a brokerage, that is given the responsibility of safeguarding the assets of a client's Individual Retirement Account (IRA). According to Internal Revenue Service (IRS) rules, an IRA custodian must be either an approved financial institution or they must secure specific approval from the IRS to act as an IRA custodian.

liens are permitted. Many financial institutions limit the type of investments they'll permit for IRAs in their custody. IRA owners who want to be invested in real estate or other non-traditional investments must find and select an IRA custodian who will permit such investments.

The message for IPSs is simple. There is a LOT of potential business you can participate in by serving investors who use their SDIRAs to invest, but only if:

1. You learn the basic rules.
2. You teach your clients how to work with their IRAs including what it takes to convert them to SDIRAs!

You do not have to become an IRA custodian to do this. You just have to establish a relationship with an IRA custodian who can help your client take the necessary steps and can advise the client (and you) what is or isn't required to comply with the regulations. It is not incredibly complicated, as evidenced by an ever-increasing number of investors who are utilizing their SDIRAs to invest in real estate, many of them investing via private syndication vehicles.

Here is a short overview of the process of teaching real estate agents and investors how to use IRA funds to purchase real estate, presented by Mr. Glen Mather, CEO of NuView IRA in Florida, who has been working hard to educate both IRA investors and real estate agents alike for many years. NuView IRA has been in business since 2003, and currently administers more than $1 billion in IRA funds for their clients.

Unlocking IRAs to Fund Investment Real Estate

by Mr. Glen Mather, CEO of NuView IRA

Another Source of Cash

Most real estate investors understand speed-to-close can often beat out higher offers that are subject to financing or other contingencies. The most attractive buyer is someone who has a high probability of getting the purchase done without it falling out of contract. That is why sellers are hugely influenced positively by cash buyers. Yet many buyers, and their agents, are not aware of the funds available to them in their own retirement accounts—resources that can legally purchase investment real estate.

Over $7 trillion dollars are currently held in IRA accounts, with millions added daily through people rolling over their company-sponsored plans, such as a 401K, 403b, and thrift savings plan, into an IRA. The vast majority of those accounts end up in accounts with IRA custodians such as Fidelity (the largest holder of IRA accounts), or perhaps Charles Schwab, Merrill Lynch, or a local bank. IRA investors have been taught that the best way, and perhaps the only way to properly invest for retirement is in the stock and bond markets. Investment professionals fail to mention that real estate may be a good choice as well. Why? Well, the advisors and stockbrokers often don't make a commission if the investor chooses this option.

Real estate investors are generally not reluctant to use their IRA to purchase real estate—they just don't know it's possible and how it is done. As an IPS agent, it is your responsibility to educate your investor about all the possible purchase options, and let them choose the best solution, as often their own tax situation is unique. As an investor yourself, it can benefit you immensely to know these funds are available to you as well.

If all the available IRA funds were to be directed into real estate instead of the stock market, there would exist a potential of more than $432 billion in agent commissions. It's time for you to get your share.

Getting Past the Doubt

Agents are encouraged not to provide tax advice, including agents who are investment property specialists. Yet, introducing a client to using an IRA to purchase property can be an intimidating subject for both the agent and client. Thankfully, there are considerable third-party information resources that can be provided to the investor that should reduce their anxiety and encourage them to seriously consider this option.

Almost all types of real estate can be purchased and held inside an IRA. Single-family homes, duplexes, apartments, commercial properties, and even unimproved land are all available options. Basically, if you can earn a real estate commission on the purchase and sale, chances are the IRS will allow it to be owned by an IRA.

The IRS has the responsibility to collect taxes according to the rules passed by Congress and signed into law by the President. The rules change bit by bit each year, and in some years, larger tax reform legislation is passed.

When it comes to the ability of an IRA to own real estate, however, the rules haven't been modified much since 1975 when the first IRA account was opened. So, for over forty years, IRA owners could have purchased trillions of dollars of real estate with their retirement plan—yet real estate agents simply didn't choose to tap into that market, and most are still are not doing so today.

The Basic Rules of IRAs and Real Estate

An IRA is actually a trust, and most agents that sell to sophisticated buyers have done transactions that involve a trust on the buying or selling side. An IRA trust is an individual retirement arrangement that is held by the trustee (normally the account holder) for his or her retirement years. If the account holder dies with assets in the IRA, they pass to the IRA beneficiary(s). The rules for the trust, including how to get money into the trust (contributions) and out of the trust (distributions), are all found in the IRS code and publications.

What are the rules of this special IRA trust? Thankfully, they are not onerous or difficult to understand—in this area, perhaps in this case only, the IRS rules follow a logical path. The IRS wants to ensure that the investment represents a true arms-length transaction. In other words, no parties involved with IRA owned assets may have a hidden agenda, a special deal cut, or otherwise corrupt a true fair exchange as if between disinterested individuals.

In an attempt to clarify the types of transactions and people who may have a difficult time engaging in a fair exchange with an IRA, the IRS has identified a list of individuals who qualify for the unfortunate title of disqualified people (DPs). These DPs are:

- A fiduciary (this may be the account holder or his designated agent who has discretionary powers—and can make decisions for the IRA)
- Certain family members of the account holder
  - Lineal ascendants and descendants and their spouses (mother, father, son, daughter)
  - Account holder spouses and ex-spouses
- Service providers to the plan (CPAs, financial advisors, etc.)

- An employer whose employees are covered by the employer's plan
- Certain company ownership provisions (generally doesn't arise with most passive real estate transactions. Your IRA custodian can explain in detail, if applicable.)

Ok, we now have a list of disqualified people (DPs)—but what are they legally unable to do? These are called prohibited transactions. Disqualified people may not:

- Buy, sell, exchange, or lease IRA owned assets
- Lend money to the IRA or use his or her personal credit to obtain a loan for the IRA
- Provide services, goods, or facilities to or from the IRA
- Transfer to or use IRA owned assets
- Benefit personally from someone providing services to the plan if they are a fiduciary

All these rules seem complicated. Perhaps you are thinking, "I'm not a tax professional. How can I determine if a real estate transaction is compliant or in violation of the IRS rules for IRAs?" Don't try. Simply speak with a professional tax advisor.

In order to assist in understanding what the prohibited transactions are, here are a few real-life examples of what a potential investor might want to do with their IRA—but which would be a violation:

- Buy an office building in order to provide space for his business
  - This would be prohibited because the IRA holder is the business owner.
- Ask the bank to loan money to his IRA and provide his vacation home as collateral
  - This would be prohibited because he cannot use personal credit to obtain financing for his IRA transactions.
- Purchase an office building with their IRA funds, then have their own management company manage it for the IRA

  - This would be prohibited because an entity that is owned by the IRA fiduciary cannot provide services to the IRA.
- Buy a condo on the beach, place it in the resort rental pool, then stay in it personally one week a year for the standard rental rates
  - This would be prohibited because the IRA owner is a disqualified party and cannot lease the IRA owned asset (despite a fair payment of standard rates).

To summarize the rules, the IRS wants to avoid insider deals, promote fair transactions, and have your IRA investments benefit you when you take a distribution, and not before. Any questions? Have your client speak with their tax professional. The self-directed custodian may also be able to provide assistance.

Titling an IRA Investment

Right from the start, if an IRA is going to purchase anything, including real estate, the IRA's ownership interest must properly appear on all paperwork, especially on all contracts.

It looks like this:

> Custodian/Administrators Name, For the Benefit of (FBO) Clients Name, Type of IRA or IRA #
>
> Or...NuView IRA, FBO Susan Heyward Roth IRA

An IRA cannot take ownership of a property that has originally been under contract with the name of a disqualified party such as the account owner. The IRA custodian/administrator will sign contractual documents on behalf of the IRA once they are initialed as read and approved by the IRA holder. Each IRA administrator may have a slightly different process, so it is good practice to contact them in advance should a client become interested in using his or her IRA to purchase property.

Financing an IRA Investment Purchase

Banks and other lending institutions always want the greatest security possible for their loans. It is no wonder that they seldom issue non-recourse loans, which are secured only by the purchased real estate rather than the real estate plus the assets of the borrower. As we mentioned earlier, a property purchased by an IRA cannot be secured by the assets of the account-holder, as that would be a prohibited transaction. But what if the lender is willing to issue a non-recourse loan? That would open the possibility of the loan, but who would be willing to take the risk if it is not guaranteed personally by the borrower?

The best source of leverage for IRA purchased real estate is the seller. After all, the seller may be the most motivated party in the transaction. Seller-financing may allow the property to be sold for a higher price, close faster, or provide special tax advantages to the seller. An IPS should always explore this opportunity because often the buyer's and seller's desires may be different than they would be in a traditional transaction.

Another non-recourse source of funds may be private lenders who are seeking a reasonable rate of return with a secured asset and consistent cash flow. Other people's IRAs are often a good source of this type of funding.

What are the terms of a loan to an IRA? It is simply a meeting of the minds—there are no prescribed terms. The down payment could be 10% or 40%, the interest rate fixed or variable, interest only or amortized, a one year bridge loan, or a thirty year traditional mortgage. The paperwork required would be a note, together with a security instrument, generally called a mortgage.

Once the transaction is complete, the IRA holder will request their administrator make payments directly from their IRA account to the lender. The IRA should have resources in the account, perhaps from tenant rental payments that provide the funds to make the mortgage payments. Should the account not have sufficient funds for the payments, the account holder, may be able to make additional contributions to the IRA account.

Can an IRA Partner with Others to Purchase Larger (or More) Deals?

The most traditional investment structure for single-family residences is fee-simple titling, which also can be used with IRA funds. However, almost all real estate ownership structures can take on IRA investors and multiple investors. Joint ventures, limited liability companies, partnerships, limited partnerships, and tenancies in common are all options for buyers.

A great way to increase the size of a potential transaction is to suggest to clients the possibility of partnering. This can be attractive to the investor for several reasons: affordability of a more attractive investment, ability to diversify over multiple purchases, or the possibility of tapping into a partner's knowledge and expertise.

Understanding Joint Ventures

IRA investors represent a broad spectrum of humanity; some want to micromanage their investments, but most simply want their funds to grow without much personal involvement. The joint venture structure permits a more passive real estate investor the possibility of earning attractive gains through combining resources with a partner who can add additional value to the investment. The best way to understand this structure is through a simple example of a rental duplex.

> Partner A has an IRA, is busy growing his business, and is friends with Partner B.
>
> Partner B is a real estate agent with a friend that runs a small rehab crew.
>
> Partner A requests Partner B be on the lookout for a duplex for sale in a nearby college town that he believes will provide a good return.

Partner B locates the property, and before an offer is placed, the partners get together and hammer out an agreement between them called a joint venture agreement (JV). This agreement can be either very simple or complex, and its purpose is to outline the obligations and benefits of each party regarding the purchase, holding, and potential sale of this duplex. Once this agreement is in place, then the real estate agent, Partner B, puts forth the purchase offer. Once the negotiations are over, the property is purchased in accordance with the joint venture. From then on, the parties are to follow the roadmap as outlined in the JV until all the elements are fulfilled and the joint venture is terminated. Here is how it might work for our Partner A and Partner B.

- Party A has $130,000 in an IRA to invest.
- Party B is willing to put in only $20,000, but will also donate his commission to purchase and sell the property, as well as manage the rehab efforts.

- All proceeds will be split 50/50 to each partner once Partner A then Partner B have their cash investments returned to them.
- Both parties want to earn a minimum annual return of 20% on this venture.
- It is anticipated that the purchase, rehab, and sale of the property will take no more than six months.
- At the completion of the rehab, if the property cannot be sold at a price that meets the stated objectives of the joint venture, it is agreed that the property will be rented out at market rates for a one year lease and the net rents will be evenly split between the parties. When that lease expires, the property will be re-listed on the MLS for sale at an agreed to price that should result in a sales within 90 days.

In this case, the negotiated purchase price is $120,000, and the IRA owner, Partner A, closes the property in his IRA. The IRA administrator signs the joint venture agreement at the direction of Partner A, and Partner B also signs. At this point, the rehab work starts, managed by Partner B. It costs Partner B $20,000 for the work and various holding expenses. At month five, the rehab is complete and the property is listed by Partner B on the MLS and is quickly purchased and closed within 30 days. The property is sold for $200,000, and after all closing costs, nets $185,000 to the joint venture.

The joint venture returns the first $120,000 back to Partner A, $20,000 to Partner B, and the remaining profit of $45,000 is split evenly between the two partners. At this point the joint venture is terminated with the IRA receiving $22,500 or an annualized return of over 37%. Partner B has a much higher return for the funds invested but had to do all the work and donated his buying and selling commission to the venture.

Both parties benefit. Partner A, the IRA holder, does no heavy lifting, just providing the capital, and Partner B, the agent, uses his expertise to find the property, fix it, and find a buyer. Partner A gets the benefit of his IRA growing without taxes, and Partner B gets the income he needs for his family, far beyond a simple commission check.

How Can I Help My Client Get a Self-Directed IRA?

Now you know that selling investment real estate to an IRA account is possible, and it appears that the deal on the table will not violate the IRS rules. Where do you point your client for more information?

Thankfully, there are a number of good IRA administrators that specialize in establishing IRA accounts that can be invested outside the traditional Wall Street offering of stocks, bonds, and mutual funds. These types of IRAs have become known as self-directed IRAs because the account holder is able to make all the investment decisions on far broader classes of assets including real estate. A good self-directed IRA administrator should be willing to educate you and your client and help make the process of purchasing property a relatively easy transaction.

Most custodians have online systems that will provide the resources to sign up electronically and direct their current administrator to transfer the funds to the new self-directed IRA account.

▶ **NOTE**

There is a seven day right of rescission from the time that the application is received before an investment can be made (meaning the client can rescind the transaction within the first seven days), so encourage your clients to open their self-directed IRA account early in the purchase process.

What Are the Administrative Steps to Buy Real Estate in an IRA?

Without a self-directed IRA account being open, no paperwork can be executed for the purchase. Once it is opened and funded, the basic steps are:

1. Fill out a purchase authorization form and submit to your IRA custodian
2. Provide a purchase contract to your custodian. They will sign on behalf of the IRA, once initialed by the IRA holder
3. Escrow information and instructions are provided to the custodian. IRA holder initials and custodian signs settlement statement and other required document

4. IRA funds are transferred to the escrow agent per IRA client's direction

From this point on, the IRA has an ownership interest in the property, and all rents paid for the property are to be sent to the IRA custodian and are posted to the clients IRA account. All expenses of the property such as property taxes, Home Owner's Association (HOA) fees, maintenance, etc., will be paid out of the IRA by the custodian at the direction of the IRA holder.

To sell the IRA-owned real estate, the above steps start with a sales authorization form and ends with a check deposited into the IRA account.

Can a Self-Directed IRA Attract More Buyers to My Business?

The good news is that real estate as an asset class is starting to gain the public's attention. Suddenly everyone wants to buy and flip as the media trumpets the successes of ordinary people creating phenomenal returns. While this picture is certainly not universally accurate, the resulting buzz has opened the door to many traditional investors being willing to listen to the prospect of owning investment real estate for the first time.

The concept of owning real estate in your IRA is still new to most people and certainly new to most agents. Having this knowledge gives you yet another significant advantage over your fellow agents. Make the message of self-directed IRAs part of all of your market messaging. Put it on your website, add an article to your newsletter, talk about it in your blog, and even put it on your business card. Host informational events and make self-directed IRAs a topic to draw in the public. Create videos or webinars on the subject or request additional information from your self-directed IRA custodian to assist you in spreading the word. The simple statement on all your promotions, "You may be able to use your IRA to purchase investment real-estate, ask me how" is all it will take to start the conversation and open the possibilities.

Just ask Les; he learned about self-directed IRAs five years ago, became interested, opened a self-directed IRA, and engaged a real estate agent to find him his first rental property. Although he has a modest IRA and is 67 years old, he now owns three properties, and his wife another, all purchased through one agent. He has no interest in moving his IRA funds back to the market, and is saving all the rental checks in his IRA to purchase a fourth property. He is also a raving evangelist for self-directed IRAs and his agent as well.

So it is clear there is lots of money to be made—more than $400 billion of commissions just sitting there in IRAs. Help your clients move their funds from Wall Street to Main Street. Harvest the benefits instead of the stock brokers while providing better results. Imagine the referrals you will get once they own investment real estate in their retirement plan!

This presentation on IRAs has been provided by NuView IRA, one of the national leaders in self-directed IRAs. For more information, you may wish to contact info@nuviewira.com or call 877-257-3296. Let them know that you learned about self-directed IRAs from Bob Helms.

CHAPTER NINE

Preparing to Become a Uniquely Successful Real Estate Agent

One way to become a very successful real estate agent is to employ techniques and strategies that distinguish your performance from that of everyone else. The most successful professionals in every discipline don't become significant achievers because they strive to be average and ordinary. Their goal is to become extraordinary and to consistently deliver exceptional results. This is only possible when you commit yourself to delivering your best and when you won't settle for anything less.

But which techniques and strategies will set us apart from other agents? How and where can we go to learn them? We can start by recognizing that good techniques and strategies need not be completely unique and that we need not be the only ones using them. One of my favorite concepts is that it isn't necessary to give natural childbirth to every good idea we decide to utilize; it's perfectly all right to adopt a workable idea from someone else who has used it successfully! It's a big shortcut!

The real estate profession is quite competitive, and as agents, we are often competing with other agents for clients, listings, and deals. Over the many years, I've been a practicing real estate broker, I've observed that many agents believe they are engaged in a business characterized by scarcity, not abundance, and this belief causes them to be very reluctant to share their ideas with other agents—their competitors. They often believe that their successes occur because of their unique ideas or methodologies, and moreover, they believe it's because they are the only successful practitioners who can and do use them. Although that is possibly true, I think there are very few ideas that are so unique that you're the only one who ever considered them! Moreover, both scarcity and abundance are much more about your attitude than actual supply and demand. My conclusion is that virtually any idea you consider using would be improved by openly discussing it with others, exposing it to the magic of synergy.

To be sure, technology provides new capabilities and helps generate new ideas and improved ways to conduct our businesses. Anything that helps us provide better service to our clients is worth considering, but be sure to recognize that the service delivered is more important than the method you use to deliver it. An email or text message or voicemail or a fax is undoubtedly more effective than a postcard for most information, but any of them is more effective than neglecting to communicate with your client. *That* we communicate with them is much more important than *how* we communicate with them!

We can dramatically increase our opportunities for success by the way we prepare ourselves. In fact, it's often stated that, "Success is preparation meeting opportunity." We must be prepared when the opportunities present themselves so we will be ready and able to take the action that's required to succeed.

Here are a few ideas that are not necessarily new, and are mostly adopted, that you may want to consider including in the list of services you provide, or incorporating into the techniques and strategies you employ.

Dress For Success

One of the most important things you can do to become a uniquely successful real estate agent is to dress for success. According to Brian Tracy, who has made a detailed study of dressing for success, your appearance is paramount in creating a successful image, and the first impression you make on others is the one they will retain of you! Moreover, they will complete their judgment about how-you-look and who-you-are within 30 seconds of meeting you! Brian offers further tips about showing up dressed for success:

- **Dress Upward:** Always err on the side of being the best dressed one there. When you look your best, people will believe that you are smarter, more attractive, and better educated, and they will retain those positive beliefs about you.

- **Dress Professionally:** If you are in a business environment, always dress professionally. For women, that means a dress or business suit. For men, that means a suit, or sport jacket and tie. Pay attention to your grooming and choose appropriate, well-polished shoes.
- **Job Interview:** Wear the clothes you'll wear if you get the job!
- **Sales Rule:** "Make it easier for the customer to buy!" Dressing appropriately will help you accomplish that mission in at least two ways. First, when you look your best, you'll succeed in creating the right impression on those you meet. Second, and perhaps even more importantly, you will be self-confident about your appearance and your ability to interface comfortably with new contacts, and that confidence will be apparent to everyone.

Here are some books I heartily recommend by Brian Tracy:

- *Maximum Achievement*
- *Advanced Selling Strategies*
- *Absolutely Unbreakable Laws of Business Success*
- *Success Is a Journey*

Apprenticeship

There is no shortcut to apprenticeship. Don't avoid it. Embrace it. Be patient. The experience you gain will help define who you become. Remember, none of us were born with the skills we ultimately need to be successful, so set your sights on getting the most out of the learning experiences you encounter on your journey of accumulating expertise.

If you can locate an experienced investment property specialist who is willing to take you under her wing and allow you to become her apprentice, look hard at the pros and cons such a position would entail. This could be such an advantage for a beginner that it seems like a complete no-brainer to me. If you can obtain a relationship where you are paid (I'd personally consider a commission share more desirable and more motivating than a salary) to participate in and learn how the business is done, it may dramatically propel your career as an investment property specialist. You might start as a transaction coordination assistant or as a new agent who helps do research, analyzes properties, solicits listing appointments with sellers, and helps prepare and present offers on behalf of her clients. The more comfortable you become with these activities and the better you become at handling these tasks, the closer you are to being able to do them for yourself.

Some senior agents build their office team by utilizing buyers agents to help them service their clients. This is a great way to break into the business because you immediately get to start with warm leads your team leader provides, thereby shortcutting the process of your finding good candidate buyers yourself.

You may also learn how your new mentor works the investment business, how she interacts with and solicits referrals from other agents in or out of your office, and how she farms for listings in the investor community. Whatever you learn will place you closer to your goal of becoming a bona fide investment property specialist. If you cannot find an opportunity for a paid assistant's position, look for other ways to trade your services for mentoring help. If working for free means that you become the beneficiary of an experienced agent's coaching, it may be the best remuneration you'll ever receive. Such a coach may not have sufficient budget to pay you, but if you can trade your assisting them for coaching, that could be a bargain! Being open to making such an arrangement could be the key to accelerating your learning curve, and fast-tracking your apprenticeship.

Client Questionnaire

The most successful real estate agents I've known have consistently been very skilled at establishing—and maintaining—great relationships with their clients. Not surprisingly, those agents are usually able to enjoy multiple business dealings with their clients over a prolonged period of time because of the exemplary service they provide. How can YOU establish such a relationship with your clients?

If you want to cater to your clients and earn their business again and again, you can start by focusing on THEIR wants and needs including helping them understand their options and opportunities in the marketplace. In order to do that effectively, it's imperative that you understand what their objectives are. I have found that creating a questionnaire (that resides in each clients file) allows me to understand that client's game plan and to keep track of their progress in growing their portfolio.

▶ **NOTE**

Prepare a questionnaire, and use it as a customized, routine service with each of your clients. This will allow you to learn what's important to each client, referrals they may need, their investment experience and property types owned, their personal investment philosophy, their target acquisitions, and their long-term goals. Are they flippers? Buy-and-hold investors? Interested in group investments (vs. individual investments)? Do they prefer passive or active roles in their ownership?

Ask them, "What characteristics or attributes are MOST important for them in selecting a new real estate agent to work with? Your goal is to "become their car company for life" (stolen from Ford Motor Co). You want to demonstrate that you are thinking ahead and that you want to be in the relationship for the long ride, not just a transaction or two! See the sample questionnaires at the end of this chapter for examples.

Create your questionnaire in your own style, but these are the primary things you need to know about your new client to provide the services they need and to be of value to them. Customize this form and add any other questions you think are important.

Keeping each client's file updated will help you determine who are candidates for transactions you create between clients. This can be lucrative, but to do this, you must know what they have, what they want, and what their long-term investment plans are. Determine how often you should review and update each of these individual investors files (I recommend quarterly) so that you are prepared to recognize opportunities that suit your clients when those opportunities appear.

These are transactions that you are in a unique position to facilitate! You can realistically create transactions between your clients that would not take place at all without you! But it won't happen by accident.

Your job is to establish a routine of revisiting each of your client's plans. Doing so will help you:

1. Regularly give them the attention they need.
2. Be prepared to help them create transactions that propel them on their intended path of improving and enhancing their portfolio holdings based on your detailed understanding of their goals and objectives.
3. Be PROACTIVE. If you merely wait for the client to call you when they next decide they're ready rather than taking initiative and presenting opportunities you've found that may work well for them now, you are not giving them the chance to take advantage of those timely opportunities. By being proactive, you're demonstrating how you bring value to the relationship by exposing them to opportunities available in the marketplace that match their stated objectives. As your list of clients expands, you'll have more opportunity to facilitate transactions directly between those clients, often without ever having had to list the properties on the open marketplace.

Sample Questionnaire for a Seller of Owner-Occupied Single-Family Residence

Seller - SFR

Do you have a home you wish to sell? ______________________

Brief description? ______________________

Where is it located? ______________________

Address: ______________________

Is your home currently on the market? ______________________

Is it listed on your local MLS? ______________________

How long has it been for sale? ______________________

Have you received offers, and if so, what happened? ______________

____

Are you satisfied with the services your real estate agent has provided, or are you considering looking for another agent? ____________________

What characteristics or attributes are MOST important for you in selecting a new real estate agent to work with? ____________________

____

Would you like to have our assistance screening and qualifying a new agent? ____

If so, we will be happy to explain how we do that and what you can expect from us.

▶ **NOTE**

If their listing is in your town, YOU are the replacement agent candidate. If it's out of town, you find the client a good referral agent to represent them and replace their current agent. Because of your background and skills, you are the best agent to help them find an out of town referral agent. You know exactly how to qualify that referral agent for them.

Sample Questionnaire for a Buyer of Owner-Occupied Single-Family Residence

Buyer - SFR

Do you know your way around our local area? ____________________

Have you had an opportunity to study our real estate market? __________

If so, have you been able to find some areas or properties you like?

____

What types of home are you most interested in? ____________________

____

How would you describe the ideal home for your family? ______________

____

(These questions and the further questions you ask lead to an understanding of the buyer's wants and needs and begin a relationship that will allow you to make an appointment to show them candidate homes to purchase.)

Sample Questionnaire for Your Investor Clients and Prospects

Are you currently interested in buying or selling investment real estate?

____

Do you own other investment properties? ____________________

What type of investment properties do you own? ______________

____

Where are your investment properties located? ________________

____

Do you manage these properties yourself or use professional property managers? ______________________________________

If you're interested in purchasing an investment property, what type of property are you looking for? ___________________________

____

When you have identified that new property, do you need to or plan to sell one of your current properties to complete the purchase? __________

If so, will you utilize an IRS 1031 tax-deferred exchange? __________

____

Is the property you will relinquish in the exchange already listed or in contract? ____

What time constraints, if any, do you have on finding your replacement property? ____

Do you have a long-term plan to acquire additional investment real estate?

____

If so, can you please tell us more about your investment goals?

____

Are you satisfied with the services your real estate agent has provided, or are you considering looking for another agent? ____________________

Would you like to have our assistance screening and qualifying a new agent? ____

If so, we will be happy to explain how we do that and what you can expect from us.

▶ **NOTE**

If their listing is in your town, YOU are the replacement agent candidate. If it's out of town, you find them a good referral agent to represent them and replace their current agent. It's important that your new investor clients know that you are an investment property specialist, that you're actively engaged in the business, and that you are an active investor too!

When searching for an investment property specialist from outside your area, you ideally want to find an agent who regularly works with other investors and is an active investor himself! A Referral Agent Profile Sheet (see Figure 5) will help you determine that agent's background and experience and whether you want to refer your client to him or keep looking for a more satisfactory candidate. If you decide to refer your client to the agent, this sheet also allows you keep track of the referral results and, ultimately, decide whether you will want to recommend using that agent again in the future.

Establishing Credibility as an Investment Property Specialist

Your goal is to become a knowledgeable investment property specialist as quickly as you can, and then, to become an investor yourself as quickly as you can.

One way to accelerate your becoming an investor is to participate with your clients in some of their deals. How can you do that?

Perhaps you can leave all or part of your commission in the property and continue to participate in the deal with your client as a junior partner. This will leave more working capital available to the operation of the property, but more importantly, will also likely guarantee you the listing agent's fee and involvement in the transaction when the property is resold. If you don't need the money to feed your family, perhaps you can "let it ride" and gain both equity and experience. This also allows you to then honestly say, "My partners and I own the XYZ Property," which begins to establish you as an investor yourself and helps establish your credibility as an income property specialist! There is no better way to gain your investor's confidence about choosing to work with you than demonstrating that you are a competent, active investor yourself!

Of course, you'll need your broker's agreement (if his share of the commission will be delayed too), but he'll likely be in favor of your plan to ultimately have more business in the future.

Real Estate Agency

Real estate agency is a complex legal subject about which much has been written and debated. The historical issues surrounding agency have to do with who represents whom, in what capacity, what commitments are made between the parties with respect to duties owed to one another, when is an agent considered to be a fiduciary, are you representing a client or a customer, etc. As you might anticipate, there is NOT universal agreement on these topics, and the debates have been ongoing for years, resulting in various "solutions" enacted into law by every state in the U.S. Some states have determined that the best solution is to utilize transaction brokers, who have only a facilitating relationship to the buyers and sellers and actually represent noone in the transaction. Well, you get the idea.

The only reason we are discussing agency is because our examples of clients and transactions in this book have primarily taken place in California. When I have alluded to being able to represent both buyer and seller in the same transaction, that is an example of a dual agency which is legal in California, but not in all states. The methods you use will be necessitated by the local customs and dictated by the laws that prevail where you are doing business.

So the question of agency is simple. You must learn what the rules are in your area and adhere to them! The department of real estate website will explain the rules you must follow. If in doubt, this is an appropriate discussion to have with your broker-manager. Be sure you understand how he or she wants you to operate and which agreements you need to have signed by your buyers and sellers for the transactions you work on.

If you happen to practice or intend to practice real estate outside the U.S. the same advice holds true about learning and understanding the laws and customs in your area. Some countries do not require a license to conduct a real estate sales business, but that doesn't lessen your responsibility to understand what steps ARE required to represent your clients' interests. "No license required" suggests that there are fewer trained agents in these countries altogether and fewer yet who are trained to handle investment properties. As a trained IPS, you will be able to command even more attention from investors if you figure out how you can help them and you provide the assistance they need. Do your homework and be prepared to answer their questions and assist them correctly so that their trust in you is not misplaced! There is limitless opportunity for those who are competent and able to provide assistance.

Certified International Property Specialist (CIPS) Designation

If you plan to do real estate transactions outside the U.S. on a regular basis, you may want to pursue obtaining a designation as a Certified International Property Specialist (CIPS) from the National Association of Realtors. This involves specialized training to ensure that you know how to handle whatever unique practices are required in the countries where you choose to practice because every country or region will have individual requirements and methods that differ from your U.S. practices.

You will be able to specialize in specific regions and countries you choose, and you will learn to handle the currencies, cultural practices, taxation issues, and of course, you will probably want to learn to communicate in your client's primary language.

Learn more about the CIPS designation from the National Association of Realtors® at www.realtor.org.

CHAPTER TEN

Habits of Uniquely Successful Real Estate Agents

Contract and Offer Strategies

Our job as investment property specialists is to help our clients select, acquire, trade, sell, and build their property portfolios as they work their way toward the real estate holdings and lifestyle they are creating for themselves. Success as an investment property specialist also includes building your own real estate portfolio as soon as you are able, so that you too, can create the lifestyle of your choice. In order to become the successful bidder for these properties, we need to develop the proper mindset for formulating and presenting our offers.

One of the most common mistakes we see, especially from beginners, is focusing on all the contingencies they think they may need to be able to get out of the contract if they find problems instead of focusing on what it takes to get INTO the contract. If you don't win the bid with your offer, it won't matter how safe and protected you were by all those contingencies! It's urgent that we learn to MINIMIZE the number and type of contingencies we include, so we can convince the seller that we and our clients are serious, real buyers who want to win, and we expect to perform. (Remember investor Robert Helms' question: "How much money will you make on property you DON'T own?") Unless you are the winning bidder, you are an observer, not a participant.

Whenever we are in a competitive bidding situation, which is most of the time, we need to look for a win-win situation for both buyer and seller and present the strongest offer we can put together. A strong offer tells a compelling story.

What Constitutes a Strong Offer?

First of all, you must absolutely do your homework. Ask the listing agent for whatever financial background they can provide (an APOD, hopefully), study the comparable properties thoroughly, and run the numbers so you may accurately determine at what price point and with what terms the property works for you or your client. If there is a property manager involved, learn whatever you can about the property's operation and the seller's motivation from them. When you submit your offer, be prepared to defend your opinion and reasoning, especially if you come in below the asking price.

How do you look strong if you're bidding below list price?

Remember that the seller is not just looking for his price. He is also looking for surety, so it's important that you show him you are ready, willing, and able to perform on the terms of your offer. To look like a strong buyer, you can:

1. Offer a large earnest money deposit. You may only be liable by state law for a 1% to 5% penalty should you default, but you'll have to come up with your full down payment in 30 to 60 days anyhow. So why not increase the deposit now to demonstrate that you are serious?
2. Get commitments from inspectors to do all inspections as soon as possible and limit your inspection period accordingly. You want to complete your "due diligence" and close the transaction as quickly as practicable.
3. Be sure to include a provision specifying that the "due diligence period" begins once all required disclosures have been provided to the buyer.
4. If you are purchasing using third-party financing, attach a loan preapproval letter to your offer.
5. If you are aware that the seller is planning to complete a 1031 tax-deferred exchange to replace this property, you should include the following statement in your offer, known as a 1031 exchange cooperation clause:

> "Buyer is aware that the seller's intention is to complete a 1031 exchange through this transaction and agrees to cooperate with the seller to accomplish the 1031 exchange, at no additional cost or liability to buyer."

Why is that necessary? Because if you DON'T include it, the seller must put it in a counter-offer, and we prefer to avoid that step, if possible. Why? To avoid, "Well, since we're writing a counter-offer anyway, why don't we also include...?"

6. If you or your client are doing a 1031 exchange as part of this transaction, be sure to include the "sellers cooperation" version of this clause in your offer. That means that if both buyer and seller are doing 1031 exchanges in this transaction, both the buyer AND the seller's cooperation clauses need to be included in the contract.

7. Pre-negotiate extensions to the contract if you anticipate delays in closing, and you may want to increase your deposit to obtain the extension. The seller will be much more likely to agree to an extension if you've provided for it up front than they will be if you've surprised them with such a request later on.

8. Be prepared to release some of your deposit money (that means those funds go hard and they are not refundable) upon reaching significant milestones in the closing sequence if necessary.

9. You have the right to assign the purchase contract to a third party, unless the contract you are using specifically forbids assignment. You may or may not be considering flipping or wholesaling the property, but that is not necessarily why we want the ability to assign it. Both you and your clients may have partners or unidentified entities your tax or estate planning attorney or CPA want you to use or create. Be prepared to discuss why assignment is routine in your business and why it doesn't represent a lack of commitment on your part. In the purchase contract and deposit receipt itself, simply identify the assignee as: "Joe Buyer, and/or assigns."

Making Successful Offers – Combining Two Powerful Ideas

We spend the lion's share of our time as real estate agents getting in position to make offers for our clients or ourselves. The degree of success we attain as an agent is directly tied to our ability to successfully prepare, interpret, present, negotiate, and council our clients to willingly enter into purchase contracts that will culminate in transferring properties into (or out of) their ownership. If we are unable to do this effectively, we will need to find a new vocation because this one won't support us in the style to which we want to become accustomed!

Indeed, if our ability to help our clients buy and sell property is a clear imperative, this is an area where we would do well to adopt or study techniques that have worked well for other agents. Here are two ideas that we have used successfully for years including an example of how to combine them in a single transaction.

Ask What Does the Seller REALLY Want?

It's easy to assume that we know what the seller of a property wants. He wants his asking price (or more); he wants it now, usually with a quick close of escrow. He'd prefer to sell it as is; he's ready to move on and be done with this property. Surely the listing agent would have told us if there were any other important considerations for the seller, wouldn't she?

While it's easy to assume that scenario to be correct, it is often a serious mistake! Many times the listing agent doesn't know what the seller really wants and is merely assuming that her seller is just like every other seller. But is he?

DON'T COUNT ON IT! If it's your seller, be sure to ask them to explain in detail what, if anything special, they really want! If appropriate, you can then communicate that information to a buyer or buyer's agent, especially if you feel it would facilitate the seller receiving an offer to which he'd be more receptive.

If you're representing the buyer, be sure to ask the seller's agent to find out what the seller really wants before you prepare your offer! This simple step can often give you the ability to structure a transaction that might not have happened without asking the all-important question of the seller. I promise you will close more deals by learning what the seller really wants!

The Erroneous Assumption Sale

Here's an example of a deal that could be described as The Erroneous Assumption sale, where Robert and I were the buyers of a fourplex we bought to upgrade and flip. Many would call this a value-added transaction. The seller was a licensed agent but listed the fourplex through another broker, and he was selling the property as the downleg of an IRS 1031 tax-deferred exchange.

So, since he was participating in a 1031 exchange, it's reasonable to assume—as we did—that he would not carry a purchase money loan for the buyer, because that loan would be considered boot and would be taxable to him, rather than tax-deferred upon sale. But, we were planning to use a hard money loan for this purchase, and we wanted the seller to carry back a 20% second loan for a short period of time to minimize the down payment required and conserve our cash for the repairs the property needed.

When we asked the agent what the seller really wanted, we learned that the seller could not find anyone willing to pay the price he wanted, so we then offered to increase the offering price in exchange for him carrying the short-term loan, which he agreed to do. The increased purchase price more than offset the seller's tax penalty and allowed him to complete his 1031 exchange. We completed the purchase, refurbished the property, and collected about $100,000 of profit when we resold the property. This was clearly a win-win for both buyer and seller.

Do you think that scenario would have ever happened if we hadn't asked, "What does the seller really want?" No, we probably would have just been stuck with our original erroneous assumption (that the seller would not or could not carry back a second loan), and there would have been no sale!

▶ **NOTE**

The topics of 1031 tax-deferred exchanges and property exit strategies are discussed in Chapter Six: How Do You Build and Manage a Real Estate Portfolio Successfully?

The Offering Summary Letter

The second technique we've used successfully for years is to submit EVERY OFFER we write to the seller and his agent with an offering summary letter (see Figure 6). This is especially important if we are unable to present the offer to the seller in person (the method we always prefer). The purpose of this one page letter is threefold. First, it quickly summarizes the highlights of the offer, pointing out the strongest features, and thereby enumerating the primary benefits of the offer to the seller.

FIGURE 6

OFFER
1234 Ideal Street, Gilroy, CA 95020
Buyer: Miss Veri Qualified

OFFER HIGHLIGHTS

- Earnest Money Deposit: $ 20,400 (3% Of P.P.)
- Down Payment: $136,000 (20% of P.P.)
- New 1st Loan: $544,000 (80% of P.P.)
- Total Price Offered: $680,000
- No Loan Contingency/ Buyer is Preapproved (Letter Attached)
- Contingencies: Inspection and Appraisal Contingencies Removed in 14 days
- Close of Escrow (COE): 30 Days After Acceptance by Seller
- Seller May Remain in Possession Five Days After C.O.E. at No Cost

ABOUT THE BUYER

Veri Qualified is the director of finance for the Really Big Money Corporation. This company's charter is to help middle-class Americans increase their net worth and obtain financial freedom prior to retirement. She has a BS in accounting and an MBA in IT from the University of Toronto.

Veri is a real estate investor, and she also operates a personal financial service business in Santa Clara County. Her strong balance sheet and her credit score of over 730 are a reflection of her financial management abilities. This is a buyer who has the income, assets and financial management skills to achieve success with any property she selects.

ABOUT THE BUYER'S AGENT

Bob F. Helms is the broker-owner of Cambridge Properties and has been practicing Bay Area real estate for over 30 years. Bob has consistently been among the top 1% of real estate producers nationwide and has successfully closed over 95% of every transaction undertaken in his long career. Bob is the former assistant manager of the Century 21 Almaden Office in San Jose.

The second purpose of the offering summary letter is that it gives us the opportunity to describe the buyer's qualifications and motivation, thereby assuring the seller that this buyer can and will perform as proposed. This addresses the issue of surety, and is meant to demonstrate that this buyer is ready, willing, and able to close the transaction, which is often more important to the seller than the purchase price. Our goal is for the seller and her agent to decide that this is the buyer whose offer they want to accept.

The third purpose of the offering summary letter is taking the opportunity to tell the seller and her agent exactly why they want to choose to deal with us as the buyer's agent. Here we are demonstrating that this buyer's agent is a seasoned professional with an exceptional record of closing transactions. In short, if you choose our buyer, you will be working with an experienced real estate team who knows how to close transactions!

If you don't personally have a lot of transaction experience, you can use this paragraph to describe your company's experience and successes, including appropriate team members' roles and contributions.

Now, let's examine the highlights of the offering summary letter more closely.

▶ NOTE

This offering summary letter example is taken directly from our files, and it was chosen to help illustrate what we include in the letter and why we do so.

---

1. **Earnest Money Deposit:** The first place we can show the buyer's strength and motivation to the seller is by making the earnest money deposit amount equal to the maximum that the laws of the state will allow the buyer to forfeit if the buyer defaults on the contract. In California, that amount is 3% of the purchase price. We could always offer a higher deposit to emphasize motivation, but the maximum amount at risk here is 3%, so that amount is commonly used to denote a ready, willing buyer.

2. **Down Payment**: In this case, we have a strong buyer with good credit. She is able to put down 20% of the purchase price, which

makes loan approval easier to obtain, and the loan process somewhat simpler and surer. While it is certainly possible to buy a home with as little as 3-5% down payment, that loan is harder to obtain. The seller knows that there is less risk of the loan not being completed because this buyer is putting down 20%.

3. **New First Loan:** The buyer is obtaining a new 80% LTV (loan-to-value) loan.

4. **Total Price Offered:** This is always important and is one of the main reasons the offering summary letter is used. The total price offered tells the seller what price and terms are offered at the outset of the presentation. In this case, the offer was made in a seller's market and this was one of five offers the seller received, all of which were higher than the list price.

5. **No Loan Contingency or Buyer is Preapproved:** Avoiding loan contingencies and obtaining buyer preapproval is especially important in a competitive bidding situation. This buyer has a full, preapproval letter from her lender, and a copy is attached to the offer summary letter, so her ability to obtain the purchase loan is not an issue. By removing the loan contingency up front, she has eliminated one of the normal contract contingencies, leaving one less step in the transaction. Without this, she would require a release from the buyer when the loan is formally approved and ready for funding at close of escrow (See Figure 7).

FIGURE 7

Bob F. Helms, Cambridge Properties

Preliminary Eligibility Approval for a Home Loan

Dear Bob,

Congratulations, we have CONDITIONALLY APPROVED your loan as requested. Based upon the information provided we have determined the loan request meets the current underwriting guidelines under the terms listed below.

Borrower:	Qualified, Veri
Purchase Price:	$680,000
Loan Program:	Conventional
Down Payment:	20.000%
Max Qualifying Note Rate:	4.750%
Property Type:	SFR, 1234 Ideal St., Gilroy, CA 95020 - Non-owner occupied

Final approval is subject to maintaining current credit and employment, additional income and asset documentation as requested, a satisfactory purchase contract, appraisal, preliminary title report and quality control review.

We are pleased to have the opportunity to assist you with this request and look forward to working with you. Please feel free to contact me at your convenience if I may be of further assistance.

Plaza Loans is a Direct Lender licensed under the CA Residential Mortgage Lending Act.

Sincerely,

Victor LoBue
(408) 472-5717 Direct
vlobue@plazaloans.com
NMLS# 345408

1155 Meridian Avenue, Suite 100 | San Jose, California 95125 | office 408.978.0400 | fax 408.978.2069
www.plazaloans.com | info@plazaloans.com | NMLS# 216565

6. **Inspection and Appraisal Contingencies Removed in 14 days:** Since the buyer's offer is contingent on obtaining satisfactory property, pest control inspections, and approval of seller's disclosures and reports, the buyer's inspection period for obtaining all such reports and releasing all contingencies is limited to 14 days, provided the inspections don't produce findings that create unresolved issues between buyer and seller. If that is the case, there may be additional inspections, or modifications to the purchase agreement.

   Appraisal is still a contingency, because even though the loan is preapproved, the loan amount the lender is willing to fund is 80% of either the purchase price or the appraised value, whichever is less. Should the appraisal come in below the offering price, an adjustment would have to be made in the price, or terms, or both, to be able to complete the purchase.

7. **Close of Escrow:** 30 Days After Acceptance by Seller: This is an important date for both buyer and seller, especially from a planning standpoint. This closing date confirms that the buyer is ready to perform in a timely fashion, and that all the steps necessary to close escrow will be done by the buyer without delay.

8. **Seller May Remain in Possession for Five Days After C.O.E. at No Cost:** WHERE DID THIS CLAUSE COME FROM? WHY IS IT INCLUDED? Well, yes...We DID ask the seller's agent, "What does the seller really want?" And she told us that they really wanted five extra days to pack, move, and clean the house before vacating. So the buyer agreed to include the five days at no cost to the seller.

   Our buyer, who was NOT the highest bidder, was awarded the contract by the seller, because the seller was convinced that she offered the best surety AND she was the only one who asked about and granted them five extra days in the property after close of escrow!

So, the use of these two simple ideas has enabled us to OBTAIN and to CLOSE many more transactions on behalf of buyers, and we learned to use both of them EVERY TIME we represented a buyer. Yes, we learned to ALWAYS ask the seller or the seller's agent, "What does the seller really want?" before writing our offer.

Systematizing Your Business

The purpose of systematizing your business is to make sure that you always take the correct actions with each client and in each situation that demands adherence to routine tasks. Your method can be as simple as establishing a template or checklist which prescribes how and which duties need to be performed and documented. Or you can actually write a manual for your employees to ensure which actions are taken, which are documented, how it's done, and where they are filed and accessed. Whichever way you choose, your purpose is to ensure that the proper response and actions are performed when needed, every time! Simple checklists can be utilized very effectively to memorialize actions or events.

An easy example of being systematized is for you or a team member to prepare a list of the items to be completed and the timetable for their completion whenever you put a new property into escrow for one of your buyers or sellers. This becomes a routine procedure that you create to ensure that the parties you represent in the transaction and your team are all working from the same schedule. It's a simple document to create, but it will save both time and promote efficiency when the party responsible for taking the action has a ready guideline to follow and can easily anticipate and perform the action items required. This escrow tracking schedule can include a checklist to ensure, for example, that:

1. The contract has been reviewed, has all necessary signatures, and that all initialed agreements are completed.

2. The buyer's check has been received and placed in the broker's account, or with the escrow officer, etc. and you or a team member acknowledged that you received It.

3. Schedules for completion of physical inspections by professional inspectors are arranged, and copies of the inspection reports are placed in the files when they are received.

4. Disclosures required from the seller are delivered to the buyer ON TIME and are filed with appropriate approvals by the buyer.

5. The buyer's loan, if any, is approved by the lender and any conditions for funding are satisfied.

6. Structural pest control inspection reports are received and reviewed by buyer and seller and an agreement is reached concerning completion of repairs and issuance of clearances.

And so forth…detailing ALL the necessary steps required for a successful completion of the transaction.

When you are systematized so that you always do the required actions and you can easily verify that they've been done, you are on your way toward doing both the required tasks and the extra tasks that ensure you're satisfied that you're meeting your client's needs and delivering your best work. Clear and easy-to-understand instructions remove any ambiguity your employees might otherwise feel, while simultaneously empowering them to work confidently to complete the tasks you want done. Consistency always pays dividends and denotes professionalism.

One way to achieve consistency and increase your capacity to handle more clients and transactions is to hire a transaction coordinator or a full-time assistant to keep you on track by assisting in routine operations and record keeping. As your quantity of transactions increases, you should begin to budget for having assistants to increase your efficiency and effectiveness. If you are able to show, for example, that your results per hour worked produces an amount of, say, $60 per hour, it's easy to justify paying an assistant $15 or $20 per hour to reduce your workload, giving you more time to do the $60 per hour tasks, while the assistant(s) do everything else. When you hire a part-time or full-time personal assistant you're able to focus on delivering more value and services to your clients.

Having your files up-to-date will also ensure that you are paid immediately upon closing each transaction, because neither you nor your broker has to wait while the missing documents are located, copied, inserted, and reviewed by the broker.

CHAPTER 10

Referrals – The Lifeblood of the Real Estate Brokerage Business

If you anticipate a long-term, successful career as a real estate agent, it is imperative that you understand the urgency—and the subtleties—of being successful at giving and receiving referrals. Simply put, referrals are your future!

Of course, it's possible for you to earn referrals from friends and family members on the strength of your personality and by being well liked! But it's a different matter when asking for referrals from other agents who depend upon your being successful for them to be successful! When you do a good job for the client that agent referred to you it's very likely you'll get additional referrals from them.

If you've done a good job for your client, it's not surprising that they will often be happy to refer you to their friends, relatives, and acquaintances. BUT DON'T COUNT ON IT! It is not automatic. You must always ASK them for referrals, don't just expect them to remember to refer you because they like you and your work. Your receiving a referral will probably always be much more important to you than it will be to them, however well-meaning they are.

Whenever I think of referrals, I'm always reminded of one of the MOST successful agents I ever worked with: Art Scott. Art was an exceptional realtor® for many reasons, and he worked his way from being an oil well rigger to becoming one of America's highest-paid real estate agents. Art and his team achieved the ranking of top ten sales agent for two of the world's largest real estate companies, Century 21 and RE/MAX. And as you might suspect, Art's business catered to high-end buyers and sellers in California's Silicon Valley. Not surprisingly, he was also an investor and an investment property specialist.

Art was a highly respected, consummate professional in the real estate business, and he was proud of the fact that referrals were ALWAYS his #1 source of new business! But not by accident!

Art actively farmed for his referrals at company conferences, award ceremonies, by email, and through postal mail campaigns just to name a few. At the national sales award conferences, every agent found a package from Art Scott on their chair soliciting their Silicon Valley referrals and offering a high, memorable referral fee of perhaps 34.567% of his commission to get their attention. Because his closing record was also very high, he usually delivered that fee to the referring agent, and the new referral segment of his business continued to grow.

Farming for Referrals Locally

Farming is not an accident, it's a plan. A farmer's crops don't come in without soil preparation, seed planting, and nurturing, and neither will yours!

A lettuce farmer doesn't really need to tell anyone what he's doing, but can just go diligently about his work to produce his crop. You, on the other hand, will have much better success telling EVERYONE about your plans and devising methods to let other agents in your office and your town know that you are looking for their referrals to their clients with investment properties. As an investment property specialist, you can help their clients with transactions those agents don't know how to do. By referring them to you, they will still be providing additional service to their clients and collecting referral fees they cannot earn by themselves.

Don't be surprised if you find agents who want to learn how to participate by becoming investors themselves. They can refer themselves to you as a client, and you can help them acquire their first properties for their portfolio. Having an active network of other income property specialists is a bonus you might not anticipate, but even though these agents are "competitors," they are also great resources in finding deals, referrals, lenders, and affiliated practitioners, and you'll want to sell their new listings to one of your clients! Think abundance! There is plenty of business for everyone, especially in this under-populated arena. An occasional slowdown or lack of sales does NOT necessarily mean there are no sales opportunities. It often means that the opportunities that exist require more time, attention, and expertise by diligent salespeople to consummate those sales.

Anytime you have the opportunity to refer your client to another agent, your job is to make sure the referred agent has the necessary skills and abilities to serve the client well. Whether they're helping your client find a property they wish to buy or selling the client's existing property, their service is a reflection of you, the referring agent. Plus, the agent you select for them is now responsible for earning his fee and yours!

Out of Town Investor Referrals

If you are doing an investor referral, your skill in finding an agent with sufficient training and experience to service your client will determine how well your client does and how well you do! Our strategy is ALWAYS to try to find an agent who is an investor themselves, because we then know that they have a much higher likelihood of success. Investor agents understand what their investor clients need.

When searching for that out of town agent, the following are some of the questions you'll want to ask.

FIGURE 8

Agent Profile Sheet

Agent: ______________________________

Company: ______________________________

Office Phone: ________________ Address: ______________

Cell Phone: ______________ Email: ________________

Website: ______________________________

Referral Source: ______________________________

How long have you been an active real estate agent? ____________

Do you regularly work with investors?____________________

Are you an investor yourself? ____________________

What types of properties do you own? ______________

What types of properties do your investors own? ____________

____

Do you have local team members you've used that you can refer our client to for: ________________________________

IRS 1031 tax-deferred exchanges? ____________________

CPA or tax attorney? ____________________________

A good local property manager? ______________________

Inspection companies that handle apartments or larger properties?

____

Are transactions in your area normally closed by your local title/escrow companies or by real estate attorneys? __________________

If it's an attorney, does your company use the same attorney regularly or will you refer the client to an independent attorney?

____

Which investor client was this agent referred to?

____

Results: ____

Client Feedback: __________________________________

Agent Referral Fees ______________________________

One important topic of your discussion with a referral agent is the compensation that you expect when they complete a transaction with your client. Referral fee amounts are negotiable, but all fees are paid to your company, not to you directly, so make sure you discuss them with your broker-manager. There may be an established referral fee policy or you may have input about what will work well in motivating that agent to perform. I have personally had good success and acceptable results by giving and receiving a 30% referral fee for both incoming and outgoing referrals, but results may vary in your neighborhood or environment. If you give and receive enough referrals, the amount of the fee will be the least of your worries.

▶ **NOTE**

Your job is NOT to micromanage the referral agent. You'll probably have little to do with that transaction, but it may require coordination on your part (such as your handling the downleg of a 1031 exchange). It's wise to pay attention so that you are aware of your client's progress for two reasons:

1. **You may need to assist them and you want to be knowledgeable about the status of their referral transaction.**
2. **This is still your client! If you expect to continue to participate in their investment transactions, you'd better be an active team member!**

I LOVE receiving referrals because they represent business I would not have without the referral. In the investment arena, I clearly expect to retain the new client and do additional transactions with them. I don't view this new referral as a single transaction, but instead as a new investor client that I fully expect to serve in multiple transactions if I provide the type and level of service they need.

How Long Do You Continue to Pay Referral Fees for the SAME Referral Client?

Great question! I am personally ready to pay fees for repeat referrals FOREVER! If I am willing to pay for a new referral, why wouldn't I want to pay a fee for a client I already know and perhaps have already done business with? If you're lucky, this will happen frequently to you. It shows that you're doing a good job handling the referral from the referring agent's point of view, and if you continue to do so, that agent will happily continue his referrals to you. In this case, more is definitely better!

Soliciting Listings – Another Art Scott story

Art Scott was a go-getter who worked at a stand-up desk (no chair). He started early in the morning six days per week after a workout at his gym. He never worked Saturdays—that was a day he spent with his two boys—and he had a trusted team of assistants, including other agents, to help him complete his tasks and transactions. Art had a daily goal for the number of prospecting calls he planned to make and he dogmatically adhered to his schedule. If he was able to complete the number of morning calls he scheduled, the team took Art to lunch. If he wasn't able to complete the target number of calls, Art took the team to lunch.

One of Art's habits was to call expired listings on the morning the listing expired to solicit the listing for his team. He sometimes called very early and occasionally angered his prospective seller, who would ask, "Why are you calling me so early?" Art's reply was, "From the lack of results you've had selling your property thus far, it looks like you need an agent who gets up earlier and works harder to get your property sold!"

Did this technique always work? No, it didn't, but within a couple hours of Art's conversation with the seller, one of his assistant's hand-delivered a complete listing package to the seller's door, with the team's marketing analysis, recommended sales strategy, and a new listing contract ready for signature. The result? Many of those folks indeed decided that they wanted to work with an enterprising team like the Art Scott team! This is a perfect example of being innovative and providing a level of service that your average and ordinary agent doesn't provide.

Becoming a Listing Agent

While I believe that referrals are the lifeblood of the real estate brokerage business, other brokers believe that learning the art of becoming a great listing agent is the most important skill you can acquire to promote longevity in real estate sales. That's a hard idea to argue against, because becoming a good listing agent ensures your participation in transactions. If you represent a buyer, you may or may not be involved in a property transaction, so you can easily see the argument for specializing as a listing agent. I don't disagree with this philosophy, but because we created a lot of transactions in which we represented both buyer and seller (both were often existing clients of ours), we didn't find it as necessary to concentrate solely on listing properties and were able to participate with lots of buyers AND sellers.

Many of our investment property listings were considered pocket listings, meaning that while those properties were not listed and actively on the market, they were available and amenable to the right offer if and when it came along. Indeed, many of the transactions we created between our investor clients took place without the properties ever being listed for sale.

This is not unusual, and in fact, we ALWAYS enjoy the opportunity to bid on unlisted properties, and much of the business conducted in the investment property segment occurs because of relationships with other principals and agents. It is not only legal to participate in insider trades and deals in investment properties, it is the preferred method of doing business! You don't need a lot of listings to participate in investment property transactions, you simply need a lot of ready, willing, and able buyers and sellers who can perform when the opportunity appears.

Sales is a RELATIONSHIP Business

It is urgent that in your role as a real estate agent investment property specialist, you focus on establishing the best personal relationship you can with your new or prospective clients. It isn't hard to make sure you take the time to ask the right questions to learn what your client is interested in, thereby helping you determine how you can best be of service to them. The old adage that people don't care how much you know until they know how much you care rings as true today as it ever has. As an agent representing your client in a transaction, you will often be creating a fiduciary relationship with that client, and this requires much more than just being honest with them. It means that you must take their best interests to heart. The sooner you are able to establish a relationship in which they "know you, like you, and trust you," the sooner you'll be able to represent them as the agent they are pleased to have on their team. And it's a two-way street because when your relationship is pleasing and rewarding for both of you, you will readily commit your time and resources to helping them achieve their real estate goals.

In the residential portion of our business, we certainly had to become skillful at promoting ourselves, obtaining our unfair share of listing appointments, and making sufficiently compelling presentations to be chosen to represent sellers as their agents of choice. Working as a team was a definite advantage because we could combine complementary skills and presentation styles, and we readily proclaimed that the Helms team offered: "Twice The Service...Twice The Results!"

When appropriate, our listing presentations included copies of our newspaper articles, special reports about the market, and oftentimes special reports concerning disclosures that the sellers were required to make to their prospective buyers. Basically, we worked hard to establish a reputation for being knowledgeable and skillful at negotiation and emphasized that our track record of successful sales and high closure rates was anything but an accident. We regularly referred listing candidates to other sellers we had represented so they could explore how well those sellers felt we had represented them and how eagerly they referred us. Of course, we asked permission before we referred new clients to our existing clients.

It is equally important that you get to know other agents in your community, whether working with owner occupants or handling investment properties, because you want to build a reputation as an agent who can be trusted and as someone who does whatever they commit to do. Because Robert and I enjoyed an enviable reputation—which we earned over an 18-year partnership—we were the recipients of many contract awards simply because agents were happy to be in a deal with us and knew they could count on us to perform. We also benefitted as investment property specialists by being contacted about other agents' pocket listings because we often had ready candidates in tow. It's important for your long-term business success to continue to build your brand, reputation, and network.

Networking is a Powerful Activity for Everybody!

If you're not a big fan of networking, GET OVER IT! It is simply urgent that you become good at this activity and that you actively seek out opportunities to meet and greet other investors, teachers, students, contractors, tradespeople, lenders, agents, and investment property specialists who can help you learn what you need to know to grow your investment property specialist business and to build your personal investment property portfolio.

Networking events provide a unique concentration of the very people you want to interface with. You will find people with whom you can exchange ideas, experiences, techniques, data, referrals. You will oftentimes find people with whom you can come together to do deals, form partnerships, and you will gain information and relationships you can use to propel both your existing and new ventures. Of course, you need to be there!

Sometimes our reluctance to attend events and relish networking is indicative of the fact that we aren't really comfortable interfacing with the very people who can help us! We may be somewhat shy or lacking confidence in our personal meeting and greeting skills, so we may feel a bit awkward and ill at ease in networking situations. It's often difficult to be confident when you're a rookie! Well, there's a great tip from Robert Helms you should try.

▶ **NOTE**

A tip from Robert Helms: If you are not "outgoing" and consider yourself shy, this is your chance to change the impression you make on others you're meeting for the first time! YOU know you're shy, but THEY DON'T, so the first impression you make on them will be the only one they have of you! Step out of your shell, give them your elevator speech AND a business card with your contact information. If you can, send them a "nice to meet you" email follow up. This is probably an ideal kind of group for an investment property specialist like you to join!

Tom Hopkins, the author of *How to Master the Art of Selling* (and the foreword of this book), asserts that very many salespeople (and we are ALL salespeople, my friends) are damaged by the widely believed myth about natural-born sales wonders. Very few think that they truly ARE that sales wonder personified, but the large majority are certain they are NOT—and they can therefore NEVER be—that natural, successful, top-notch salesperson of myth. They therefore unconsciously sabotage their own potential accomplishments. If we believe our performance is in the hands of fate, then we need not be responsible for our performance or for our failures! But when we accept the responsibility for our own performance, our mantra becomes, "If it's to be, it's up to me!"

Self-confidence is really about your attitude. If you have studied the things that are important to you and you have become COMPETENT in your subject matter, your attitude will reflect your CONFIDENCE. The more you know about topics that interest you, the better your ability to discuss and interface with others about those topics will be. Having the ability to contribute to others is an amazing elixir which will serve you well as your confidence in your ability increases.

Leads Clubs: A Great Source for Referrals

A very good source of referrals can be from the members of a leads club or another networking club that is specifically organized for the purpose of providing a forum for members to meet, interact, and learn how they can refer business to each other. A leads club normally allows only one member from each category (realtor, lender, hairdresser, health spa operator, attorney, etc.). This results in all referrals to the hairdresser going to the same member each time.

Robert and I received regular referrals from a leads club attorney specializing in family law for sales of probate properties, and we became good referral sources for each other's businesses. The leads club met for breakfast each week, discussed our business ideas and strategies, and worked seriously at providing leads for the other group members. It was relatively inexpensive and effective for most members who were consistently able to provide client leads to one another. By the way, the member who consistently gave the most referrals was Joanie the hairdresser! Each year someone was awarded the "Joanie" trophy for producing the most referrals!

There are also leads clubs that welcome multiple members from each discipline, and they devise their own methods of lead distribution. I think it's more important that you provide each other leads than how you distribute them. Recognize that whenever you receive a referral from someone, that constitutes a third-party endorsement of your services and your character, so the referring party is definitely recommending you as the best person for the job. The required action on your part is clear, "Do a good job, and you can keep it!"

▶ NOTE

CAUTION: Our leads group received an application for membership from a pest control operator, and upon checking his credentials with the state licensing board, we determined that he used to be licensed, but wasn't currently licensed. Obviously, that's a problem, and we declined his application. If the member you refer people to for goods and services is required to be licensed to legally operate their business, it would be prudent for you to determine that requirement, and

perhaps require that the club keeps a copy of appropriate licenses and permits on file, and renew those copies whenever they are updated or reissued.

There are multiple formats for leads groups, and depending upon the size of your city or town, you can either find a leads group you like or consider starting your own group. What you are after, of course, is the opportunity to network with other business owners or employees who can and will refer you to prospects for whom you can provide your services. If there are no leads groups in your town, check larger MSAs (Metropolitan Statistical Areas) to see what is being offered, who runs it, whether the city chamber of commerce is a supporter or endorser of the group, etc. From my experience, this is a worthwhile endeavor to pursue. You might start with your own chamber of commerce to find an existing leads group.

At least one nationally chartered group, Le Tip, has been in existence for many years and its members are generally long-term and very satisfied with their referral process. Find out if there is a Le Tip or other club near you that you can visit to get a first-hand understanding of how they work and how their members feel about their participation. Visit www.LeTip.com!

An internet search for leads clubs will uncover several leads organizations who offer help in forming a leads club in your area.

Real Estate Investment Clubs

Most larger communities have one or more Real Estate Investment (REI) clubs that offer education, networking, an organized structure and meeting place, and the opportunity to meet active investors, as well as affiliated tradesmen (flooring, carpeting, plumbing, roofing, painting, and electrical contractors).

There will be rules of conduct about how and when you can meet and socialize with other attendees (you can't just stand in the hallway passing out business cards), but these clubs perform a vital function, especially for newer investors, and they are highly recommended for agents who are investment property specialists.

Not only will you have the opportunity to see who the other investment property specialists in town are (if they come to the meetings), but you'll also learn how other local investors and agents view your marketplace and make good connections to help you navigate and gain a foothold in the club itself. Don't wait until you've been a member for five years to become involved in the club's activities. Volunteer to help with meetings, expos, and conferences so that you become known and can contribute to and benefit more from participation in the club.

In larger cities, some of the REI clubs are large enough to sponsor their own real estate expos. Sometimes several clubs band together to do so. Their conferences attract many local and national sponsors who operate booths to display their wares and skills as well as local and nationally known speakers who share their knowledge and experience. If you're a new agent and haven't yet built your team of affiliated practitioners, attending an REI club event will be a good step to meet potential mentors, service providers, and other candidates for your team. Be prepared with business cards, a short 30-second elevator speech about who you are and what you do, and be ready to network!

For information about joining or forming a new REI club, go to www.REIClub.com. Their directory will show you the location and contact information for REI clubs throughout the United States and Canada. I was intrigued to learn that there presently are 9 REI clubs in Canada, while the U.S. has 10 states with NO clubs, 18 states with 5 or more clubs, and 4 states with 12 or more clubs! The greater Los Angeles area alone has about 25 REI clubs!

NARPM

NARPM is an acronym for the National Association of Residential Property Managers, which has chapters in most of the major cities across the United States. This organization is comprised of active residential property managers (PMs) who manage everything from single-family homes (SFRs) to larger multifamily apartment buildings as well as many affiliated tradesmen who perform the maintenance and repair operations needed to keep their many rental units in good operating condition. I recommend you check to see if there is a NARPM chapter in your area because you may want to become a member. Visit www.narpm.org.

Because NARPM offers training and certifications to their property managers, they tend to have well-educated broker members managing properties. This makes them a good resource for obtaining real information about their local marketplace. I personally have three brokers, each of whom has been the president of their NARPM chapters, who have managed properties for me or my clients. All three offer exceptional service. Many of these brokers are also investors and investment property specialists who list and sell properties for the property owners. However, others choose to specialize in property management only. They will refer their listings to other agents when their clients want to sell, buy, or exchange properties. You might become their referral agent if you pursue that option, and being a NARPM member could serve you well. For example, who do you use now to repair gas ranges? Who installs carpeting for you? Who do you refer your clients to for property management? Your local NARPM chapter can provide all those services and service providers!

Retaining Clients

We are talking about the many ways you can find, engage, and serve your clients. As your client base grows, so does your opportunity to do more business. It stands to reason that some thought must be given to retaining the clients you have worked hard to find. Many studies have shown that the cost and effort necessary to retain an existing client is far less than it is to find and secure a new one.

Even so, a surprising number of agents put very little effort into servicing their existing clients between transactions. It doesn't really take much effort to send updates or special reports on the marketplace, notice of relevant seminars, notices of new tax or investing rules, or maybe simply sending a birthday card to all your past clients. It allows you to stay front and center, and it's especially important with investors, who can generally do another transaction whenever you find a good candidate property and bring it to their attention!

Here's a simple procedure that real estate trainer and investment property specialist Walter Sanford suggests that is easy and effective. Walter keeps a file of HUD-1s (essentially the closing documents for your client's purchase or sale of a property). Walter's staff inserts a copy of the closing docs for EVERY property sold throughout the year into this file. Then in early January of each new year, they send each of their clients a fresh copy of those docs to help them report the sale or purchase when preparing their income taxes for the previous year. This is simple, effective, and a service virtually no one else provides. It doesn't take a lot to stand out, but it does take planning and some effort.

If the client perceives that you continue to provide value to him, your chances of continuing to do business together are obviously improved. You have at least a slight edge in retaining your relationship if you provide a little extra effort and show a little extra care.

The Primary Complaint of Clients

Do you know what the primary complaint was from clients who decided not to do business with the same agent they used last time they did a transaction?

"I never heard from him again after the transaction was completed."

WOW. And here the agent was thinking he'd get some referrals from that client, but he didn't even get hired again to represent that same client this time!

Let's make sure we get the lesson here. Losing a client due to inattention is completely avoidable, and is an easy problem to prevent. Make sure it doesn't happen to you; all that's necessary is for you to provide a periodic touch and evidence of your interest in the client. It's not hard, but few agents do it. Here is another chance to stand out among your peers, but more importantly, to retain your hard-earned clients!

▶ NOTE

Add reminders to your calendar to send them HIC (How's It Coming?) cards, birthday cards, emails, HUD-1s, copies of notes, deeds of trust, leases or other actionable items created in their transactions, invites to seminars you or associates conduct, updates on comps and opportunities that show up, and articles about investment topics, etc.

IF IN DOUBT, SEND IT!

Newsletter or Blog

Consider creating a newsletter or a blog which you send regularly to all your clients by either email or regular mail. This is a great vehicle to deliver timely or important data, market trends, meeting notices, and more which will serve to keep you connected to your clients while reminding them about your services. Offer to refer them to other professional practitioners (attorneys, CPAs, lenders, service companies, IRA custodians, contractors) as needed and invite them to email, fax, call, or meet you to answer any questions they may have pertaining to real estate. This is also a good vehicle to highlight skills, responsibilities, and accomplishments of your employees and team members so your clients may get to know them too.

CAUTION: If you elect to do a newsletter or blog, it will be most effective if you do it regularly, and continuously rather than irregularly or sporadically.

▶ NOTE

A very easy and very important tip is to use a proofreader to screen EVERYTHING you offer to the public. If you write anything which is meant to impart information to others, they will NOT be impressed with typos, misspelled words, syntax anomalies, or other errors. These errors are easily avoided, but if you don't correct them before they go out, it allows your reader to form the impression that you are careless in your work habits so maybe it's not a great idea to put too much trust in your offerings! Like it or not, you only get to make ONE first impression. The reputation you want with your clients is hard to earn, so don't tarnish it with unintended mistakes that are easily corrected.

Create Your Own Website

If you are a tech-savvy IT type, you can probably set up your own website, but no matter who actually creates it, your website is an important tool to distinguish you from the proletariat! Your 80-year-old clients may not be as particular about how you communicate, but your 30-year-old clients will definitely prefer to communicate by telephone, texting, or email over "snail mail." (By the way, don't ignore the importance of knowing how to communicate effectively with those 80-year-olds. They usually own LOTS MORE real estate than the 30-year-olds!)

Establishing your own website will make sure you Google, Yahoo, and Bing well, which will help people who wish to know who you are and how you present yourself actually find you. Your website can emphasize education, areas of expertise and experience, and can highlight your current listings, the property types you specialize in, and who your associates or team members are. It can also contain information about you and the activities you wish to promote.

You can feature a regular newsletter or blog on the website, and can feature writers from your industry affiliations on a rotating basis, if you are in need of additional content. It's also possible to hire inexpensive ghostwriters to research or write copy for you on almost any subject you choose, on a daily or weekly basis.

There are numerous website design companies available to help you create your website, and yes, all of them are easily found online. The cost varies depending on whether you use a predesigned template or original artwork and layouts. You'll need to decide what works best for you based on the content you want and whatever budget constraints you determine are satisfactory. Whatever you decide, use your website to describe who you are, what you do, and why so many people choose to do business with you.

▶ **NOTE**

Make sure that you design a website that is responsive and mobile friendly or you will lose up to 50% of those 30-year-olds because they won't be able to read the full page on their small cell phone screens!

This chapter has focused on the habits that uniquely successful investment property specialists employ to ensure that they deliver their best work. If you are determined to take advantage of the phenomenal opportunity that is in front of you, you'll find it a far simpler task if you adopt the idea of replicating these proven habits which successful agents have spent years learning and utilizing to maximize their productivity. While there is always room for creating new ideas and methodologies, few strategies are more effective than utilizing the power of good habits.

Recommended Reading List

1. *The Power of Habit* by Charles Duhigg
2. *Smarter, Faster, Better* by Charles Duhigg

GLOSSARY OF TERMS

1031 TAX-DEFERRED EXCHANGE: A provision in the tax code which allows an investor to defer capital gains tax due upon the sale of an appreciated investment property by using the equity in the property to purchase another income property (or group of properties). There are a significant number of rules to be followed when executing a proper exchange. You should work carefully with your tax advisor and an experienced 1031 tax-deferred exchange intermediary when planning and executing a 1031 tax-deferred exchange.

ACCELERATED DEPRECIATION: The tax code provides the opportunity to accelerate depreciation on certain items related to your property. For example, while a two-unit residential income property structure (the building) may be depreciated over 27.5 years, there may be personal property and other items that can be depreciated much faster—only five years in some cases. When the depreciation schedule is shorter, each year's depreciation and the resulting deduction are much larger. This will improve your cash flow. You should review this concept with a qualified, experienced tax advisor. Accelerated depreciation can help you more comfortably handle the cash flow on an income property in the early years of ownership, when cash flow can be most challenging.

ADJUSTED GROSS INCOME: AGI is the amount of income you have which is taxable. It is determined by taking your gross income minus all of your allowable deductions. AGI is important to real estate investors because passive activity loss eligibility is based upon AGI.

AFTER TAX CASH FLOW (ATCF): This is the amount of net cash flow remaining after paying all required and currently due income taxes. Work closely with your tax advisor on this because depreciation schedules and passive activity loss rules change from time to time.

AMORTIZATION: The gradual pay down of a loan balance. Each monthly pay down contains both pay down of a portion of the principal (the original borrowed amount) and interest. The portion of the payment that reduces the principal is what we call "amortized equity." Amortization is not tax-deductible.

APOD: Short for annualized property operating data, this is a detailed cash flow analysis of an income property. It takes into account income, expenses, and debt service. It is the profit and loss statement of a rental property.

APPRECIATION: One of our absolutely favorite things! Appreciation simply means the value of the property is going up.

ARITHMOPHOBIA: An acute and paralyzing fear of arithmetic, a phenomenon named by Russ (Spreadsheet) Gray which dominated his early childhood.

BALANCE SHEET: A balance sheet is the financial statement that tells you what your net worth is. Assets (what you own) minus liabilities (what you owe) equals net worth. Since one of the primary objectives of investing is to grow net worth, the balance sheet is an important tool in tracking progress.

BASIC INCOME FORMULA: This is the calculation used to determine the net operating income of an income property. The formula is gross scheduled rents minus operating expenses equals net operating income.

BEFORE TAX CASH FLOW (BTCF): This is the amount of cash flow an income property generates, taking into account income, expenses, and debt service, but not considering income tax.

CAPITAL GAIN: The positive difference, or profit, between the total acquisition cost and net sales price of a property.

CAP RATE: Short for capitalization rate, cap rate is a percentage that shows how much net operating income a rental property produces relative to its purchase price or fair market value. It takes into account operating expenses, but not debt service. Cap rate only accounts for return from operating income, and not from appreciation, depreciation or amortization.

CASH FLOW STATEMENT: An investor's cash flow statement is a very important tool. It shows income and expenses from all sources. If expenses exceed income, the shortfall must be met from one's balance sheet—either through liquidation of assets or increases of liabilities (debt).

COMPARABLE MARKET ANALYSIS (CMA): An estimate of fair market value determined by comparing the subject property with other comparable properties (comps) in the area. Unlike an appraisal, which is a more formal analysis based only on past sales, a CMA also takes into consideration current listings and pending sales. CMAs are typically generated by real estate agents as a free service to prospective clients as part of the agent's marketing program.

DEBT SERVICE: The amount of monthly payments required to pay for a loan or loans.

DEED OF TRUST: See Trust Deed.

DEFERRED MAINTENANCE: Required maintenance that has not been performed.

DEFLATION: A phenomenon that occurs when the amount of money in circulation decreases relative to the supply of goods and services. Even when there is demand to buy things, if there is inadequate purchasing power in the economy, prices decline. This sets off a chain reaction of loss of profits and jobs. If allowed to continue unchecked, deflation results in recession, and in severe cases, economic depression.

DEPRECIABLE BASIS: The amount of the cost of a depreciable asset such as a rental property, to which the depreciation schedule is applied. Your depreciable basis can be adjusted during the term of your ownership as you invest in the property. Work closely with your tax advisor and keep good records.

DEPRECIATION: An accounting term which accounts for the gradual deterioration of a capital asset held for the production of income. In the case of real estate, it is the improvements (the structures) on the land which deteriorate over time. The tax code makes provision for a property owner to deduct this "loss," which does not necessarily require any actual out-of-pocket expense by the owner. Real estate investors enjoy depreciation because it provides non-cash losses, which can be deducted against real-world income. As a side note, both the income and losses generated by income property are passive. For information about depreciation and passive activity loss rules, refer to IRS publication 925 available at www.irs.gov.

DUE DILIGENCE: The research a prudent investor performs when evaluating markets, properties, and service providers. In terms of investment real estate, most contracts should contain a clause which permits a period of time called the inspection period for this research to take place.

EARNEST MONEY: A check included when a potential buyer submits a real estate offer as a show of good faith.

EQUITY: One of our favorite words, equity is the net value of a property. It is the difference between the fair market value of a property, and any debt owed against it.

EQUITY PARTNER: A co-investor who shares the risk and reward of ownership, as opposed to a lender, whose risks and rewards are limited. Typically an equity partner brings cash into the deal, but sometimes other contributions such as property, effort, credit, materials, etc., can be counted as purchase equity.

FLIP-AND-HOLD: The technique of buying a property then quickly refinancing it to get all invested capital back out without relinquishing the property. In other words, you flip the cash but hold the property for long-term total returns.

FORCED EQUITY: The equity an investor receives from proactively adding value through new development, rehab, or conversion as opposed to simply waiting for the property to appreciate due to limited supply, increasing demand, and increasing capacity to pay.

FOUND EQUITY: The equity an investor immediately obtains simply for buying the property as opposed to the passive equity that occurs gradually over time or forced equity for which the investor must proactively add value to the property itself. Not all properties have found equity, though we certainly wish they did.

GOOD WILL: The positive feeling people have toward you and your business. It is the thing that gives a business value over and above the actual financial value of the business's assets.

GROSS EFFECTIVE INCOME (GEI): The ACTUAL rents collected from a rental property after adjusting the gross scheduled income for bad debt and uncollectable rents.

GROSS RENT MULTIPLIER (GRM): A ratio between the gross scheduled income (GSI) and the purchase price or fair market value (FMV) of a particular income property. GRM is determined by dividing the FMV of the property by the annualized GSI.

GROSS SCHEDULED INCOME (GSI): The amount of income a rental property is capable of bringing in when it is fully rented and without vacancy or delinquency. It does not take into account any expenses or debt service, but simply shows the maximum potential gross income based on current leases. Also see Pro Forma.

HARD MONEY: Funds obtained from private (non-institutional) lenders who specialize in making real estate backed loans. Typically the loans are expensive in terms of fees and interest rates and are made through loan brokers who specialize in working with distressed borrowers (people who have poor credit, little income, or some other condition which makes conventional lenders refuse to lend to them). Investors like to use hard money lenders because the lending criteria are much more liberal, and loans can get funded much faster. If there is enough profit in a deal, the interest rate and fees on a hard money loan are justifiable.

HUD: A United States government agency. HUD stands for Housing and Urban Development. HUD is a great source for real estate statistics. For more info visit www.hud.gov.

IDLE EQUITY: Equity in a property that is sitting on one's balance sheet, but that is making very little contribution to cash flow or equity growth. Too much idle equity is one of the biggest mistakes investors make.

IMPROVEMENT RATIO: The percentage of the acquisition cost of a rental property that represents the value of the improvements. For example, if a property were purchased for $100,000, and it was determined that

$80,000 of the value of the property was the building (the improvements to the land), then the improvement ratio would be 80%.

INVESTMENT PROPERTY SPECIALIST (IPS): Although not an official designation recognized by the National Association of Realtors®, becoming an investment property specialist who can assist investors in the acquisition and sale of investment real estate can propel you to that coveted echelon of top-earning real estate agents worldwide. You must learn the skills illustrated in this book by becoming fluent in speaking income and learning to help your investor clients understand the many advantages of investing in real estate. Whether they invest in the U.S. or in one of the many other countries that offer exceptional opportunities for financial returns, you absolutely have the ability to become their go-to investment property specialist!

LIMITED LIABILITY COMPANY (LLC): A statutory entity, like a corporation, which exists to shield the owners from the liability of the venture. Conversely, an LLC can be used to protect an asset held by the entity. Like a partnership, an LLC provides for two primary classes of shareholders (known as members): managing members and limited members. A managing member can be a non-owner and is actively engaged in the operation of the business or management of the asset. The limited member puts up only money and has no active role. In exchange for this passive role, the entity limits the potential liability of the limited member to only the loss of any money invested by the limited member.

LISTING: When a seller signs a contract with a real estate broker to market the seller's property, it is known as listing the property. The marketing contract is called a listing agreement or an exclusive right to sell agreement.

LOAN-TO-VALUE (LTV): A percentage of debt relative to the purchase price of a property. For example, if an investor places $10,000 cash down on a $100,000 piece of property, he would need a loan of $90,000 to complete the acquisition. A $90,000 loan against a $100,000 value would be 90% LTV.

MORTGAGE: A two-party debt instrument secured by real property. The two parties are the borrower and the lender. In the event of a default on the loan by the borrower, the lender may foreclose through a judicial procedure. Aside from the legal, technical differences, there is very little real-world difference between a mortgage and a promissory note secured by a deed of trust. In most discussions of real estate financing, the term mortgage is commonly used.

MULTIPLE LISTING SERVICE (MLS): The database of properties listed for sale by Realtors® (members of the National Association of Realtors®). Sharing this information is a cooperative effort of regional agents through a local board of realtors so that any given property is given as much exposure to potential buyers as possible. Prior to the internet, this was a powerful and exclusive tool. Even today, properties which are listed on the MLS tend to sell faster and for more money than those properties which are not listed.

NEGATIVE AMORTIZATION: When a loan payment is insufficient to pay the entire amount of accrued interest, the unpaid interest is added to the loan balance. For example, if a property had a $100,000 loan on it at 6% interest, the annual interest expense would be $6,000 and the monthly interest expense would be $500. If the borrower only paid $300 on a particular month, then $200 of unpaid interest for that month would be added to the unpaid loan balance of $100,000, and the new outstanding loan balance would be $100,200.

NET OPERATING INCOME (NOI): A calculation used to analyze real estate investments that generate income. Net operating income equals all revenue from the property minus all reasonably necessary operating expenses.

NOTICE OF DEFAULT: In certain jurisdictions, a legal notice filed by the lender when a borrower has defaulted on the payment terms of their loan. It is a public notice that alerts the world that a foreclosure procedure is beginning. It also warns the owner to cure the default or face foreclosure.

OPTIMIZATION: The balancing of maximum financial result against other important considerations. For example, if an investor were to optimize the portfolio for equity growth, he would use the maximum amount of leverage possible without taking more cash flow risk than he is willing to. Because each investor's circumstances vary, the maximum amount of leverage available to a borrower may not be what is optimal. What is optimal is very personal and will emerge as an investor develops clarity in their goals and personal investment philosophy.

OWNER CARRY-BACK: A situation when the seller of a property accepts a promissory note secured by the subject property via mortgage or trust deed from the buyer in lieu of cash. Though sometimes difficult to find and negotiate, seller financing can be a very effective way for a buyer to preserve cash on the front end of a transaction and for a seller to attract a buyer in a slow market. Owner/seller financing is sometimes advertised as OWC for Owner Will Carry.

PASSIVE ACTIVITY LOSS (PAL): A tax term that describes the operating loss on a property. PAL is calculated on federal tax form 1040 Schedule E and, based on the taxpayer's eligibility, may be used to offset earned or passive income. For more information on this important topic, visit www.irs.gov and read Publication 925.

PASSIVE EQUITY: A term we use to describe the increase in fair market value of a property held over time. It is equity for which the investor does not need to do anything other than own or control the property as it appreciates.

PERSONAL FINANCIAL STATEMENT: A document that presents your assets, liabilities, and net worth.

PHASED EQUITY: The passive equity which accrues to an investor in a new development project that is being released to the market in phases when, at each phase, the developer raises the price. When an investor buys into this type of development in the early phases, the programmed price increases of the later phases actually raises the value of the investor's early phase purchase.

POINTS: Interest and commission paid at the origination of a loan. A point is 1% of the loan amount.

PRIVATE PLACEMENT MEMORANDUM (PPM): Primarily a disclosure document that is more descriptive than persuasive in style which allows a potential investor to decide on the merits of the investment. It specifically addresses both external and internal risks facing the proposed venture and should disclose concerns a prudent investor wants to be aware of before committing funds to the project.

PROFIT AND LOSS STATEMENT (P&L): An accounting of income and expenses. However, depending on the method of accounting, a P&L may be different than a cash flow statement. When expenses and income are being accrued (counted when earned or owed rather than received or paid) a P&L might not precisely match a cash flow statement.

PRO FORMA: A fancy word to describe financial projections that are based on "reasonable estimates." In the real world, pro forma can sometimes be synonymous with made up. Be careful when looking at a pro forma. Make sure the numbers are based on something close to reality by verifying the assumptions used whenever practical.

PROMISSORY NOTE: A note signed by a borrower in favor of a lender and a contractual promise to pay back money borrowed. In real estate, a promissory note is typically secured by pledging the subject property as collateral for the loan.

REALTOR: A licensed real estate salesperson who belongs to the National Association of Realtors®, the largest trade group in the United States.

ROI: Short for return on investment. In the strictest sense, ROI is only calculated on the amount of actual cash returned on a particular investment. Return implies a return of cash. When cash isn't being returned, we use equity growth rate and total return to describe how fast one's wealth is growing.

SEASONED: In some cases, experience, and in all cases the passage of time. In the case of conventional real estate loans, they are considered seasoned when the loan has been in place for six months to one year, depending upon the new lender's guidelines.

STOCK: Short for stock certificate or shares, stock is simply a piece of paper evidencing ownership in a corporation. Stocks are sometimes referred to as equities, because you own a piece of the corporation. Stocks can be publicly traded or privately held, but most investors deal in public companies whose stock is traded through the various stock exchanges (New York, NASDAQ, etc.).

SYNDICATE: An association of individuals formed for the purpose of conducting and carrying out some particular business transaction, ordinarily of a financial character, in which the members are mutually interested. Syndicates may exist as corporations or partnerships (either general or limited).

Source: *Black's Law Dictionary*

STRUCTURED SALE: Also known as an ensured installment sale, a type of sale which can be used for the sale of either a business or property and that combines the tax deferral benefits of an installment sale with the surety of a structured annuity to ensure that taxes are paid as funds are received rather than being due upon sale. A structured sale may also be a backup plan for a seller who cannot find a replacement property to complete his 1031 tax-deferred exchange.

SYNDICATION: A real estate syndicator (or sponsor/manager) is one who gathers investors into a group for the purpose of buying, operating, and ultimately selling income-producing property—hopefully realizing a profit to share in doing so. The primary difference between the syndication buying an existing property or building a new ground-up development is that both the risks and the rewards are higher with new developments.

TAX LIEN CERTIFICATE: A certificate of claim against property that has a lien placed upon it as a result of unpaid property taxes. Tax Lien Certificates are generally sold to investors by most counties and municipalities in the United States through an auction process.

TAX SALE: The forced sale of property by a governmental entity for unpaid taxes by the property's owner. The sale may be a tax deed sale or a tax lien sale. Under the tax lien sale process, depending on the jurisdiction, after a specified period of time if the lien is not redeemed, the lienholder may seek legal action which will result in the lienholder either automatically obtaining the property, or forcing a future tax deed sale of the property and possibly obtaining the property as a result.

TOP-LINE REAL ESTATE: A term to describe the gross value of an investor's real estate holding irrespective of equity or debt. In other words, the aggregate value of all the real estate owned or controlled.

TOTAL RETURN: Our term to describe the total amount of growth experienced on a real estate investment, particularly an income property, when taking into account income, amortization, passive activity loss, and appreciation. Some people like to use internal rate of return (IRR), but I find it a confusing term. We just want to know what a given investment's total amount of contribution to one's overall finances is when all aspects of contribution (cash flow, amortization, appreciation, depreciation, etc.) are taken into consideration.

TRUST DEED (TD): A document signed by a borrower which secures a promissory note on real property and authorizes a third party, typically selected by the lender, called a trustee, to auction off the subject property in the event the borrower fails to make payments according to the terms of the note. Although not technically correct, many people simply refer to trust deeds as mortgages. In the real world, the terms are virtually interchangeable. We just say mortgage.

YIELD MAINTENANCE: A prepayment penalty that, in the event the borrower pays off the loan before maturity, allows the lender to attain the same yield as if the borrower had made all scheduled mortgage payments until maturity.

PAST GUESTS INCLUDE:

Robert Kiyosaki
Steve Forbes
Denis Waitley
Mark Victor Hansen
Peter Schiff
Kevin Harrington
Dave Liniger
Donald Trump
Herman Cain
G. Edward Griffin
Ken McElroy
Jim Rohn
Tom Wheelwright
Darren Hardy
Kathy Fettke
Dave Zook
Chris Martenson
Simon Black
Beth Clifford
Kyle Wilson
***And* Bob "Godfather" Helms**

21 Years on Radio & Counting...

Robert Helms — Founder & Host
Russell Gray — Co-Host

Authors of *Equity Happens – Building Lifelong Wealth with Real Estate*

The Real Estate Guys™ Radio Show is a talk program for real estate investors and has been broadcasting weekly on conventional radio since 1997. The podcast version of the show is heard in more than 190 countries, and is one of the most downloaded investing podcasts on iTunes.

Subscribe to our weekly podcast on 

www.RealEstateGuysRadio.com

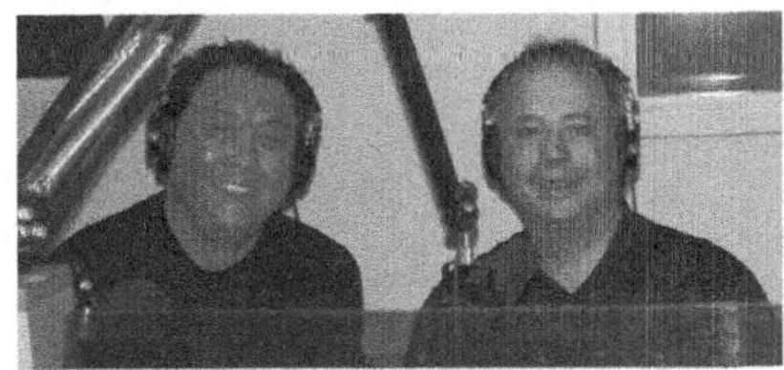

"If you are serious about investing in real estate, listen to The Real Estate Guys. They really know what they're talking about."

-Robert Kiyosaki

Best-selling Author of "Rich Dad, Poor Dad"

ABOUT THE AUTHOR

What do you call a man who has been investing in real estate since 1957, has been a practicing real estate broker since 1980, and has been a powerful mentor to Robert Helms, Russell Gray, and hundreds of others in his lifetime? We call him "The Godfather of Real Estate." Most people know him as Bob Helms.

In his career, Bob has owned, managed, bought, and sold hundreds of properties for himself and his clients. He has been both a top-producing agent and a managing broker overseeing sales agents in a thriving real estate office. Bob has probably forgotten more about real estate than most people will ever know. Yet, well into his 70's, Bob continues to practice real estate both as a broker and an investor and he remains an avid student of the business.

Bob's wealth of professional knowledge and personal experience have made him a featured contributor to The Real Estate Guys™ radio and TV shows, as well as a popular speaker at live events and The Real Estate Guys™ annual Investor Summit at Sea™. More than anything, Bob loves people—and he enjoys getting to know them as much as he enjoys sharing his wisdom.

Bob is passionate about challenging real estate agents to serve real estate investors and dramatically increase their earnings from commissioned sales while also learning to invest for themselves!

Made in the USA
Columbia, SC
27 December 2018